Humane
Pressure Point
Self-Defense

By
George A. Dillman

With
Chris Thomas

A Dillman Karate International Book

First published in 2002 by:
Dillman Karate International, Publishers
251 Mt. View Rd, (Grill)
Reading, PA 19607
USA
www.dillman.com

ISBN 1-889267-03-1

15,000 copies in print

A NOTE TO THE READER

This book is written as a means of preserving a vital, historical aspect of the martial arts. Dillman Karate International, Publishers, and the authors make no representation, warranty or guarantee that the techniques described and illustrated in this book will be effective or safe in any self-defense situation or otherwise. You may be injured, or you may injure someone else if you train in the techniques presented within. We therefore suggest that you practice only under the supervision of a qualified instructor and exercise the utmost restraint in training. Dillman Karate International, Publishers, and the authors are in no way responsible for any injuries which may result from the practice or use of the techniques presented within. Some self-defense applications illustrated may not be justified in some circumstances under applicable federal, state or local law. Neither Dillman Karate International, Publishers, nor the authors make any representation or warranty regarding the legal or ethical appropriateness of any technique mentioned in this book.

ACKNOWLEDGMENTS

We would like to thank the many people who have made this book a reality. Thanks to Wendy & Tom Countryman for principal photography; to Tom Countryman for layout and artwork, and to Kim Dillman for photography, editorial advice, and proof-reading. Special thanks to acupuncturist Ed Lake and police sergeant Bruce Fronk for technical assistance, and to Matt Hayat and George Buse for help with research. Thanks to those who appear in the photos: Reese Boyd, Bill Burch, Tammy Burch, Adam Caswell, Kim Dillman, Debbi Dillon, Greg Dillon, Lydia Bender-Dillon, Harvey Flesburg, sergeant Bruce Fronk, officer Travis Pobuda, and Dave Poirier. Special thanks to Wally Jay, Remy Presas, Seiyu Oyata, and the late Hohan Soken for the knowledge they have shared. And thank you to all the worldwide members of Dillman Karate International for your support and encouragement.

TOP LEFT: Authors George Dillman and Chris Thomas.

ABOVE: George Dillman and Bruce Lee in 1967.

BELOW: George Dillman with Todd Senefonte (stunt double for Jean-Claude Van Damme).

The authors with actor Ken Moreno, whose screen credits include: *The Fugitive*, *U.S. Marshals*, *Natural Born Killers*, *Chain Reaction*, and *Soul Survivors*.

Tae Bo founder Billy Blanks with George Dillman, on the set of the sci-fi action movie *TC 2000*. Dillman was one of Blanks' karate instructors.

George Dillman and Benny "The Jet" Urquidez. Urquidez is a world-famous kick-boxer who had a featured role in the film *Grosse Point Blank*.

David Carradine, star of the TV shows *Kung Fu* and *Kung Fu: The Legend Continues*, with George Dillman.

LEFT: Well-known martial artist and stunt actor Eric Lee, with Ed Lake.

BELOW: Lake demonstrates a technique while teaching a seminar on Dillman Pressure Point Method. Eric Lee can be seen in the background matching his movements.

LEFT: Wally Jay and George Dillman

BELOW: Leon Jay, George Dillman, and Leo Fong.

The Dillman Karate International website is at www.dillman.com.

Leon Jay, Remy Presas, Paul Bowman, and George Dillman in London. Presas and Dillman were in England conducting seminars.

Over 150 martial artists attended the 1999 Dillman Karate International Summer Camp, held in Indianapolis. The three-days of intensive training featured instruction by George Dillman, Kim Dillman, Chris Thomas and Ed Lake.

Muhammad Ali and George Dillman trained together at Ali's Deer Lake, PA, training camp in the early 1970's.

Muhammad Ali and Kim Dillman mugging for the camera in 1972.

Muhammad Ali in a karate stance. Ali sparred with many black belts, and was so good at karate point-fighting that Dillman awarded him a black belt.

In 1997, George and Kim Dillman bought Muhammad Ali's old training camp, to use for seminars, meetings, and as a Bed & Breakfast.

TABLE OF CONTENTS

INTRODUCTION

As our world becomes increasingly violent, the need for simple and effective self-defense increases. At the same time, the need for humane self-defense has increased even more.

Lawsuits are becoming a common way of shifting blame and extorting money. As a result, the old adage, "Better to be judged by twelve than carried by six," becomes increasingly less apt. A person who effectively protects life and limb in a moment of violent attack, may be sued by the very same attacker, and subjected to years of legal and financial torment. This can occur even if a jury brings an acquittal in a criminal case. The laws in this country allow for a person acquitted in criminal court to still be sued in civil court.

This need for a humane form of self-defense is especially strong for people who are defending themselves against those whom they are hired to protect. For example, patient-care nurses and police officers have a legal obligation to defend themselves using the least amount of force required.

Furthermore, individuals who need self-defense skills are generally those who do not want to actually harm another human being. To blind an attacker with an eye-gouge is a simple and effective form of self-defense. But, most people of good conscience find this to be morally abhorrent. As a result, they would hesitate before using such a method — even in a life-threatening situation. That hesitation virtually guarantees that they would become a victim should a violent encounter occur.

So, how can good people defend themselves and their families in a manner which is both effective and humane? We believe that the answer lies in the traditional martial arts. We believe that the ancient warriors of Okinawa, who developed the art known today as karate, possessed the knowledge of just such a method. The method is called **kyusho-jitsu**, pressure point fighting, and it was kept secret for many years. In the last few decades, certain karate masters of the "old school," worried that these secrets were in danger of being lost, began to share this intimate knowledge. Having been fortunate enough to be introduced to these methods, we have devoted ourselves to researching and sharing the techniques of pressure point fighting.

We believe that these methods can make an excellent contribution to our society. Pressure point techniques require little strength (though some skill); yet, can easily incapacitate a larger, stronger assailant, without causing serious injury. This makes the art especially appropriate for those who are the likely targets of aggression, while being a means of self-protection that can be employed in good conscience.

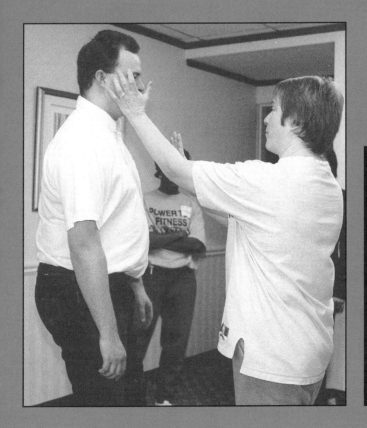

G eorge and Kim Dillman travel the globe teaching seminars on *Humane Pressure Point Self-Defense* to martial artists, police, security personnel, and civilians. The photos on this page — and others scattered throughout this book — were taken during a training session taught for the staff and security force of a major hotel in downtown Toronto.

Caution:

Humane Pressure Point Self-Defense **is intended as a means of self-protection that is not harmful to others. Nonetheless, it still must be practiced with restraint and the utmost respect for any training partners.**

In order to enjoy the maximum benefit, study Dillman Pressure Point Method under the careful supervision of a qualified instructor.

CHAPTER ONE: Principles of Self-Defense

PART I: KNOW YOURSELF AND YOUR ATTACKER

To practice effective and humane self-defense, you must: a) Know yourself and understand your attacker; b) Be utterly committed to protecting your own life, and willing to do whatever it takes to prevail; c) Comprehend strategies which can make it easy to overcome an attacker; d) Have a working knowledge of the bio-mechanical principles which will allow you to succeed even when you are outmatched; e) Train in the use of the pressure points and vital targets that will stop an aggressor.

The famous strategist Sun Tzu said, "If you know yourself and know your enemy, you cannot be defeated." Thus, the first step in self-defense is to know yourself and understand the nature of your assailant. Generally speaking, the targets of violence can be divided into two types: those who are willing to do whatever it takes to survive (survivors), and those who are not (victims). Generally speaking, attackers can be divided into four categories: the Career Assailant, the Deranged Attacker, the Bully, and the Intoxicated Acquaintance.

VICTIM OR SURVIVOR?

How do you react when people behave badly towards you? Do you take it? Do you believe that you deserve it? If you were ever attacked, did you cooperate with your attacker in the hopes that submissive behavior would placate him? And if so, how did that make you feel?

Ask yourself these questions:

- **If you came upon a man assaulting your spouse, child, or some other precious person in your life, would you be willing to do absolutely anything to that man to protect your beloved?**
- **Would you be willing to stab that assailant with a knife?**
- **Would you be willing to smash his head with a cast iron skillet?**
- **Would you be willing to poke a sharpened pencil into his eye?**

If your answer is no, then throw this book away. If you are not willing to do whatever it takes to save someone you love, then you will never be able to defend another person, much less defend yourself — even humanely!

If however, your answer is yes, then ask yourself these questions:

- **Why should you hesitate for even a moment to use the same methods if you are the one being assaulted instead of your loved one?**
- **Aren't you are every bit as valuable as your beloved?**
- **Don't you deserve the same utter commitment to protection?**

You do not deserve to be victimized by anyone, and if you are assaulted, you deserve the most determined and effective self-defense there is.

This is where self-defense breaks down. People say they are willing to fight for another, but they are not willing to fight for themselves. Somehow, they have come to the conclusion that they are not worthy of defending. This is a lie: You are worth defending by any and every means possible. And even if you cannot believe in your own value, consider the consequences to your family if you are assaulted and perhaps killed. How would they feel if you were murdered? How would they feel if you were raped? For their sake, if not for your own, you must be willing to fight, fight, fight.

THE FORCE FIELD OF INTENTION

Simply the willingness to fight can be a powerful deterrent — almost like a force field — which an assailant can sense on an instinctive level, as the following example illustrates: One day, author Chris Thomas heard some commotion between a man and a woman. Unable to tell if the woman was being physically assaulted, he went to investigate. When he got close, he found the woman to be visibly upset. "Are you all right?" he asked. At this intrusion, the man started toward Chris, making verbal threats. As the man approached, Chris began talking calmly and soothingly. Inwardly, Chris had determined exactly how close he would allow the man to come before he would knock him unconscious. In his mind he drew a "line in the sand."

As the man was nearing that line, Chris was saying, "I see a man yelling at a woman, I check to see if she's all right, and I think you would too." Inside, however, he was mentally preparing to strike. The man walked right up to, but not past, that invisible "line in the sand" and stopped as if he had hit a wall. Then he slumped, said, "Yeah, I guess you're right," and walked away.

This book focuses on humane self-defense — on techniques that can effectively stop an attacker without causing serious bodily harm. But, these techniques will be largely useless for you unless you are willing to go beyond them and fight as viciously and ferociously as possible.

Humane fighting tactics require commitment and confidence. If you hold back for fear of injuring your attacker, you will be the one injured. If you are afraid that your technique will not work, then it won't. But, if you are willing to start gouging eyes and biting off noses to defend yourself if necessary, then you can use humane tactics successfully.

An attacker is willing to do anything to you. He is not concerned about moral issues! You must be utterly ruthless in defending your own life, or the life of your loved ones! It is a paradox of fighting that in order to fight humanely you must first be <u>willing</u> to fight inhumanely.

THE CAREER ASSAILANT

The Career Assailant approaches an assault with a calculating manner. He understands physical violence as a means to obtain an outcome (usually, your purse or wallet). Such an individual will strike from behind without warning, and — unless you are psychic — you won't see it coming.

Your very best defense against the Career Assailant is common sense. Avoid environments where they might lurk. Keep your doors and windows locked. Do not advertise possessions which thieves might want to steal. Make sure your home is well lit (Career Assailants hate the light and love the shadows). As you approach your car, scan the area, including under your vehicle. Do not get into your car without first checking the back seat to make sure it is empty. Travel in groups, especially at night. Do not allow strangers to stand closer than nine feet from you (in law enforcement this is called the Reactionary Gap; see page 164), even when you are helping them by giving directions. Do not approach a strange vehicle. And **NEVER ACCOMPANY A STRANGER TO ANOTHER LOCATION** (more on this later).

If you are held up by a Career Assailant, you have a good chance of surviving unharmed if you simply hand over cash. From a self-protection standpoint, it is helpful to keep $100 or so on your person as insurance in the event you are robbed. Divide the $100 and keep it in two locations (such as coat pocket and pants pocket). When robbed, simply hand over the money from one of the locations. Then, say, "Hang on, I have more," and hand over the rest. The robber is satisfied because he scored $100, and he perceives you as very cooperative and helpful. You, on the other hand, have survived a life-threatening situation and it only cost you $100 (not a bad deal).

Sometimes the line blurs between the Career Assailant and the Deranged Attacker (described below), such as: the case of a strung-out junkie committing armed robbery in order to get a fix. In these cases, handing over the cash can still be your best bet. However, an additional strategy is to throw the money to the left, and run away to the right while shouting "Fire" at the top of you lungs. To the attacker, picking up the money and leaving will generally seem like a more attractive option than chasing after you.

THE DERANGED ATTACKER

The deranged attacker is an individual so enraged by fear, chemicals or mental illness that his actions are irrational. The violence pours out and seems to have a life of its own. Do not try to reason with him, or figure out how to calm him down. His thought processes are crazy, and you, as a sane individual *CANNOT* figure them out.

In some ways, whether you fight back against a deranged person or not is almost irrelevant to him. Something has set him off, and you have become the target of his insanity. Perhaps fighting back will cause him to become more violent. Perhaps cooperating will cause him to become more violent. You can never know. Therefore, in such cases it is best to fight back as fiercely as possible and do everything in your power to escape to safety.

THE BULLY

The most common assailant is the bully. The bully is lazy and uses the threat of violence — more than violence itself — as a tool of control. He counts on the fact that you will be too "polite" to react at the first sign of threat or inappropriateness (out of fear of appearing rude). But, if you remain passive at the first sign of threat, it will become increasingly more difficult for you to reverse that decision and take action, even when the level of intimidation increases. Soon you will become a victim, paralyzed with indecision and fear. Once this occurs, the bully easily controls the situation, deriving a perverse pleasure from his domination. Bullies come in all shapes and sizes, but they all follow the same basic procedure: "Intimidate, then perpetrate."

For many, the bully is a member of your own household, perhaps an older sibling, an abusive parent or a violent spouse. Even in these domestic settings, the bully uses the same pattern of intimidation to produce paralysis. The difference is that the process can be stretched over months and years. Once you have adopted the pattern of not defending yourself against the bully, it becomes very difficult to change that decision. Fighting back begins to feel impossible.

Instead, you will expend an enormous amounts of energy trying to avoid "setting him off." But, this is impossible. Despite what a bully will say, (e.g. "Why do you make me punish you like this?") the triggers for the violence are entirely internal and have absolutely nothing to do with you.

The best course of action when dealing with a bully (even in cases of domestic violence) is to fight back from the beginning. Even a physically stronger bully will think twice if he knows that every time he assaults you he will get hurt too. A good attitude to have is this: You may beat me up, but I'm going to make it cost you something. (This does not only mean fighting back physically. The same thing can be accomplished by leaving the relationship and/or pressing charges.)

PREDICTING VIOLENCE

In many ways, the techniques presented in this book represent a failure in self-defense. When a person is actually engaging in the physical act of self protection it means that he or she has failed to recognize an imminent threat and take action to escape or abort it. Well known security expert, Gavin DeBecker, describes the warning signs and predictors that one has been targeted for violence. As a matter of reference, we briefly mention here those warning signs and we strongly recommend DeBecker's book, *The Gift of Fear*, as essential reading for anyone who is interested in self-protection.

1. Forced Teaming: An assailant seeks to create an attachment or partnership — a sense of "we" — with an intended victim. This allows the assailant to get close and to create an artificial sense of trust.

2. Charm and Niceness: In our culture, there is the false belief that someone who is polite and charming is a "good" person. An assailant will use this expectation to cause an intended victim to lower her/his guard.

3. Too Many Details: When attempting to mislead an intended victim, an assailant will often use talk, and especially use "too many details" to appear as if he is open and friendly. A skillful liar uses details to create the appearance of honesty and truth (as beautifully demonstrated in the film *The Usual Suspects*) and to create the illusion of being someone with whom the intended victim is familiar.

4. Typecasting: Typecasting means to slightly insult an intended victim so that she/he feels compelled to disprove the accusation by cooperating with the assailant.

5. Loansharking: An assailant will often do an unbidden favor for the intended victim as a way of making her/him feel obligated or indebted in some way.

6. Unsolicited Promise: An assailant will make an unsolicited promise to a potential victim as a way to reassure her/him and quiet natural suspicions. An unsolicited promise in any setting is a sure sign that the person making the promise is trying to convince *you* to do something *he* wants.

7. Discounting the Word "No": It is sometimes said of men that they take the word "No" not as the end of the discussion, but as the beginning of a negotiation. If this is true of men in general, it is particularly true of assailants. This is a very important warning sign, and women in particular would do well to learn to say the word "No" with forceful clarity (after all, many a would-be rapist has been schooled on the foul adage, "When a women says, no, she really means, maybe.")

THE GIFT OF FEAR:
Survival Signals That Protect Us From Danger
by Gavin DeBecker
Little, Brown and Company, 1997

In other words, self-defense against a bully — all kinds of bullies — can be very simple: just fight back. If you are a potential target who is too difficult to control; if you struggle instead of cowering; you will be too much bother for the vast majority of bullies. The following true story is a perfect example:

An assailant entered a woman's home and grabbed her. He threatened her life and she became paralyzed with fear. Suddenly, she thought of her daughter in the next room. Finding the resolve to resist in the instinct to protect her child, she began to fight back. She hit at her attacker with elbows and feet. During the scuffle he threw her into a wall. Clearly she was outmatched. Her attacker was a physically stronger male who had the ability to defeat her. However, instead of pressing his advantage, the assailant ran from the house.

In essence, the woman lost the fight, yet, she won the battle because of her willingness to defend herself and her daughter.

THE INTOXICATED ACQUAINTANCE

In addition to the three types of serious attackers who maliciously intend to harm you, there is also a fourth type. It is the friend or neighbor who simply becomes aggressive and inappropriate after too much alcohol (or other substance). Such attackers are as dangerous to you as the others. But, they lack a hurtful intent. Once sobered up, they might even be ashamed and apologetic about their behavior. But while intoxicated, they could easily cause you serious injury.

These attackers are the most difficult to deal with. In the case of the deranged assailant, the career assailant, or the bully, you might be willing to do anything it takes to defend yourself. Against a drunk acquaintance, you would likely find yourself especially restrained by a desire not to cause them harm. The techniques in this book have the potential to deal with serious attackers in an efficient and simple manner. They are also designed to do so in a way which will cause little or no harm. This means that the very same techniques can be used against that drunk neighbor, preventing injury to him and to you.

However, the best strategy for dealing with the intoxicated acquaintance is simply to remove yourself from the environment. Make a decision not to be in any situation where someone is behaving badly. Leave — or ask that acquaintance to leave — the minute it becomes clear that a problem is developing, but before it actually does arise.

If leaving is not an option, then use your voice. Tell the drunk to back off. Enlist the help of others in this. Alcohol may cause a person to be aggressive with one individual, but if there are several people telling him that his behavior is inappropriate, even a drunk will listen. Oftentimes the people around you are feeling the same way. But, they haven't found the courage to speak up. If just one person says something, others will find themselves voicing their agreement.

PART II: STRATEGIC PRINCIPLES OF SELF-DEFENSE

The following are some self-defense strategies which, when properly employed, can greatly increase your chances of surviving if you are ever attacked.

1. Be resolved to defend yourself. All assailants are predators and like their animal kin, they know how to spot the easy target. So, if you are not an easy target, you probably won't be attacked. Your willingness to fight to defend yourself is a powerful tool. Predators can sense this and are more likely to leave you alone. If they do attack, they are more likely to be hesitant and tentative, giving you a better chance of escape.

2. "If you wish to attack west, first attack east." This is an ancient proverb, and one of the most important concepts in self-defense. In essence, you are trying to make the attacker want to do what you want him to do. If you want to free yourself from his grasp, make him want to let go. If you want to escape, make him want to push you away. The goal of self-defense is to survive and escape. Yet, the best way to do that is to attack your attacker with as much determination as possible. Soon, your attacker will be pushing you away. When that occurs, you will be able to make your escape.

For example, if someone grabs your wrist, and you try to pull your hand away, you will soon find yourself in a tug-of-war. If instead you give him a bloody nose with your free hand, he will let go. If an attacker puts his hand on you in a sexual manner, don't knock his hand off. Instead, trap it to your body and bend one of his fingers back sharply. He will be desperate to let go.

This concept of "attacking east" can be applied in another way. If you go directly for a self-defense technique, you may find your assailant resisting you. If, however, you do something else first, you take his mind away from your primary objective. This makes it easier for you to complete your technique.

For example, if your best hope of defending yourself in a given situation lies in grabbing the attacker's head and using a head turning technique to throw him to the ground (see Chapter Two), you could first kick him in the leg. Distracted and unbalanced by your kick, he will be unprepared to resist as you grab his head.

3. Make your self-defense response a conscious decision. Even though we are advocating a physical response to an attack, only you can decide what is appropriate for the situation you are in. While we believe that fighting back is the best approach in the vast majority of cases, there are certainly times when compliance is the only way to survive. However, it is important that you make the choice — a real and conscious choice — about the best course of action.

If you do not fight back when you are attacked because you are paralyzed by fear and indecision, you will have a very hard time recovering from the emotional trauma. If, however, you do not fight back because you make the conscious decision that cooperation is the only way to survive, you will still be able to work on other forms of self-defense. Pay careful attention to your attacker. Remember details that you will be able to report to the police. If possible, collect physical evidence, such as some of the attacker's hair. If possible, scrape some of his skin under your fingernails. Actively look for things that you can use to help in his apprehension and arrest. This is as much a part of self-defense as kicking and striking.

4. The best self-defense is awareness and avoidance. Avoiding potential danger is more important than defending yourself if you are attacked — common sense is one of your best weapons. Stay out of circumstances where assaults are common. Be aware of your environment and of areas of potential danger. Pay attention to who is around you. If a person or a situation makes you feel uncomfortable, leave. Do not worry about appearing rude or impolite — trust your gut. Often your instinctive awareness of danger will warn you long before your thinking mind can recognize a problem.

5. Your voice is a weapon. Do not forget that there are non-physical ways of avoiding or preventing assault. It is often possible to protect yourself without acting physically. Verbal strategies are one approach that can be used. If a stranger is acting in a threatening way, you might suddenly introduce yourself (use a false name) then ask, "What's your name?" As a conditioned response to the question, the potential assailant may actually tell you! Suddenly, you have forced this person to see you as a human being, and not an object. You have also obtained information which is useful should you end up reporting an assault to the police.

   You might try speaking in a parental tone and saying, "You ought to be ashamed of yourself," or, "I know your mother!" Simply a strong *kiai*, or karate shout, might startle someone enough to dissuade them from attack. You might act insane or psychopathic. You could make yourself throw up (on the assailant!), or cough and sneeze in a disgusting manner. Do anything you can think of to cause your assailant to change his mind about attacking you, or to at least hesitate long enough for you to make the first strike and escape.

6. Act first, act decisively. When physical force is necessary, make the first decisive move. One very important truth of combat is this: if you are close enough to touch someone, you are close enough to hit them, and there is absolutely nothing they can do about it! The reverse is also true: they can hit you and you cannot prevent it. Fortunately, the most common types of assailant — the bully and the intoxicated acquaintance — usually enter into range for a first strike (by you) before they actually begin using physical force.

   The bully uses fear and the threat of violence before he actually victimizes. Part of this strategy involves maneuvering inside the intended victim's "personal space." By getting close, he can make a person feel unsafe and insecure. But, from a strategic standpoint, he actually brings himself into range of your preemptive attack. While he

DEFENSE WITHOUT FIGHTING

The most humane form of self-defense arises from awareness and confidence, and involves no physical violence, as the following story illustrates: One night, author George Dillman and his wife Kim were out at a karaoke club, when suddenly a stranger made aggressive moves towards George, saying, "What you looking at?" This is a common barroom tactic intended to create indecision, fear and inaction in a potential target.

"I'm not looking for any trouble," said George. "My wife and I are just here to enjoy the karaoke." George did not look away or retreat. He made no threatening or aggressive gestures, his tone and demeanor were placating and calm, but inwardly he was resolved and willing to fight if necessary. Confused, the man left.

A few minutes later, he returned with a pool cue, which he leaned against the bar. Clearly, he was placing a weapon nearby. Once again, he resumed his verbal harangue on George. Up to this point, Kim had been careful not to speak or interfere in anyway. This time, however, she took action. Rising from her seat, she calmly took the pool cue and walked away with it. The man's confidence was destroyed at the sudden loss of his weapon. The lack of fear shown by George, and the awareness exhibited by Kim, helped him to recognize that he was clearly in over his head. At that point, he left.

Some time later, he returned again. This time he apologized for his behavior, and offered to make amends by buying George a beer.

is busy trying to intimidate you, you can seize the opportunity to make the first move. Remember, "Action is always faster than reaction."

Under the influence of alcohol, the intoxicated acquaintance lacks awareness of proper space and distance. Those who have had too much to drink invariably lose all sense of boundaries and inappropriately move too close for comfort. (Who hasn't had a drunk friend breathing into their face?) This means that when the intoxicated acquaintance begins to act aggressively, he is already in range for your strike.

The conclusion then is this: if an aggressor is close enough to hit you, make sure you hit him first. Sometimes, when there is a fight between two individuals the question is asked, "Who threw the first punch?" Ethically, the person who hit first is not necessarily the one who started the fight. Trust your instincts. If a person has insinuated himself too close to you and you feel threatened or uncomfortable, take action. Firmly tell him to back off. If you feel the situation warrants it, hit him and make your escape.

On the other hand, if an assailant is outside your reach do not enter into a kickboxing match with him. Instead, leave. If you cannot escape from the situation, use guile to win. You can pretend to be afraid and intimidated. This can cause him to become overconfident, while you lure him closer. He will never see your attack when it comes.

If the situation warrants, you can play along, or act as if you are sexually attracted to the assailant. Stroking an attacker's cheeks can really be a way to move your hands into position to attack his eyes, or ears. Pretending to want to kiss the attacker can bring you into range to bite him. (However, bear in mind that biting someone can expose you to any blood-born pathogens — such as HIV or Hepatitis — that he might carry.)

7. Never go with an attacker!! And teach your children to never go with an attacker, no matter how he threatens. Sometimes an assailant will wave a weapon menacingly and say, "Come with me or I'll kill you." This means that he intends to kill you anyway, once he gets you someplace he considers safe. But, the setting in which the abduction is taking place is not where the perpetrator has enough control to commit his crime. If you go with him, he will take you to a place where he can do anything he wants to you, and there will be no one to help.

So, if someone attempts to abduct you, do not cooperate. Instead, scream, yell, kick, fight and most of all, RUN. If a perpetrator does not feel safe victimizing you where you are, he probably won't feel safe pursuing you as you try to escape.

Never surrender advantage! Author Chris Thomas discusses the practical application of the principle. Even though the assailant is on the ground, one more technique may be necessary in order to insure your safety when you flee. In this case, a stomp-kick to the Lower Leg Point (see Chapter Three) can cramp up the attacker's leg, giving you time to escape.

8. Never surrender advantage! To escape from a violent encounter you must create some window of opportunity — some advantage over your attacker's intention. As soon as you have that advantage, act upon it. Most strategic opportunities will last for several seconds. This is long enough to capitalize on the situation, but not long enough to wait or hesitate.

For example, in Chapter Two we describe a simple finger control that can drop virtually anyone to the ground — even a child can perform it on an adult. However, once an assailant is on the ground, he won't stay there. So, the opportunity to escape exists only until he can recover his wits and rise to his feet. If you are still there when this occurs you will have more trouble.

Do not assume that the presence of other people will protect you. We all know stories of people doing nothing — not even calling the police — while a woman is brutally assaulted outside their windows. And, what if the incident occurs at a party? Another guest acts violently, and you drop him to the ground counting on the social pressure of the other guests to protect you from further action by your attacker. Sure enough, in humiliation, he leaves the party. But, odds are he is waiting outside to ambush you and "get even."

9. Never play the game of escalation! In a confrontation with an assailant, it is almost certain that the attacker has some kind of superiority in the situation. This can include larger physical size and greater strength, the willingness to harm you, a weapon, companions, surprise, and more. If you incrementally increase the level of confrontation, but never end it, your assailant will always have more advantage to draw on. At some point in the escalation process, you will have reached the stage where you are no longer able (either emotionally or physically) to escalate further. At this point you have run out of options, while he is still in control.

Part of the reality of escalation is that the human organism reacts more to the *difference* in intensity than to the *degree* of intensity. If someone is slapping you, then they slap you a bit harder, you do not notice that slight increase because you have been desensitized by the preceding events. If, however, you are slapped without warning, or if, after being slapped lightly you are punched, you will be physically and psychologically unprepared to receive the blow. Sudden, unexpected outbursts of verbal or physical violence, or sudden and unexpected changes in the level of verbal or physical resistance have the greatest effect.

This means that once you have made a decision to take physical action in defense of your person, you must act decisively and without warning. If you consider self-

THE MYTH OF THE "FAIR FIGHT"

People sometimes talk about fighting fair when they discuss self-defense. Good people have often felt that, if they were ever in a fight, they were never to cheat. However, this concept is a complete myth. Consider professional fighters. The two fighters in a ring are matched as nearly as possible in terms of weight and skill. It would not be considered a fair fight if a boxing world champion were put up against a novice. Nor would it be considered a fair fight if a 5' 2", 110 pound woman were placed in the ring with a 5'10", 170 pound man. But, in a self-defense situation, this is precisely what happens.

An assailant is not looking for a fair fight, he is looking for an easy target. He actively seeks victims who not only could not beat him in a fight, but who he feels will not fight at all. And, the less confidence he has, the more likely he is to try to increase the odds in his favor by using a weapon. Therefore, it is extremely important not to think in terms of "fighting fair" or "fighting dirty." Self-defense is about survival and escape. If you live, you have won. If you live, and your decisive action in your own defense allows you to feel that you have achieved a personal victory instead of becoming a victim, you have won double. The truth is, *Humane Pressure Point Self-Defense* is not really presented here for the sake of the assailant. It is not them we hope to protect — it is you. We want you to be able to defend yourself effectively, and not feel that you were reduced to savagery to do so. We want you to survive with your dignity and your self-respect intact.

defense options as a scale, with verbal defense near the lowest end, and the application of lethal force at the highest, then it is important to always jump two or three steps in escalation in order to obtain the desired results. The assailant must be unprepared for the intensity of your response.

10. Face your attacker. It has been observed by military historians (Grossman, 1996) that in pre-modern warfare, there were not many deaths until one army turned away and began to run. At that point the killing would begin in earnest. In a fist fight, it can be observed that the first blow is usually thrown when the victim looks away (for any reason) from the aggressor.

Apparently, the majority of human beings have a psychological resistance to committing violence when facing their victim (the hood placed over the face of a condemned man is for the sake of the executioner). This resistance disappears virtually the instant the victim turns away. So, if you are being threatened and you turn to run away, you actually increase the likelihood of violence against you. While running away is the ultimate goal of humane self-defense, you cannot actually make your escape until you have created an opportunity to escape safely. Until that point, face the attacker and do not turn away from him. Furthermore, if you are being chased down by someone, it is best to turn and face him before he overtakes you.

It should also be noted that you can predict the moment of attack by the act of turning away. If you are facing a threatening individual, fixed in your resolve not to turn away, and your assailant turns away from you, he is very likely about to attack. Since you do not look away from him, he looks away from you so that he is not seeing your face at the moment he commits to violence. A simple solution is this: any time an aggressive individual turns away from you, take one step back. If he does attack, he will attack where you were and not where you are.

A special point should be made of this when you are with a companion who is suddenly faced with an aggressive assailant. For example, if a woman and man are at a bar, and suddenly somebody "gets in his face," she may want to help the situation by taking his arm and saying, "Come on, honey, let's just go." However, by doing this, she has actually endangered him in two ways. First, by grabbing his arm, she has reduced his mobility. Second, he will likely look away from the opponent and turn to speak to her in response to her actions. The moment he does this, he will most probably be hit.

Another situation where this point should be considered is when you are approached by a stranger. An individual who intends to attack you, may walk right up and say, "Do you know what time it is?" Without thinking, you look down at your watch and get hit. The best technique is to lift your watch up to your face, so it is between you and the stranger. As you look at your watch, you are still facing him, and thwarting his attack. In general, be wary anytime a stranger tries to get you to look at something so you are not facing him.

11. Take action at the first sign of a threat. If you feel uncomfortable or threatened you are probably in danger. Millions of years of evolution have fit you with very sensitive intuitions. They can be trusted. The moment you begin to feel threatened your body will begin to react. Adrenaline will begin to flood your system to prepare you for "fight or flight." Adrenaline is one of nature's powerful tools. It can provide tremendous and unexpected strength when needed. However, adrenaline is a chemical of *movement*. If you begin to get the adrenaline flood, but you do not move, your body will freeze up and feel weak and shaky. Your mind will also freeze up. So, the moment you feel threatened, <u>move</u>. It almost doesn't matter what you do, as long as you do something. Some options include pacing, talking with extensive hand gestures, raising your voice. Any physical movement will help prevent you from becoming paralyzed by your own protective mechanism.

SELF-DEFENSE IN RELIGIOUS THOUGHT

The traditional martial arts have had a long association with religion. In Europe, the concept of chivalry owed much to Christian teaching, and some chivalric knights — such as the Knights Templar — regarded their martial skills as a form of religious vocation. In China, kung fu has long been connected with various temples — in particular the Shaolin Temple — and closely allied with pious devotion. In Japan, the teachings of Zen-Buddhism were a major influence on the martial arts, so much so that all forms of martial arts, including karate, are regarded as a form of "Zen-in-motion". One martial art in Japan, Shorinji-kempo (which is the Japanese pronunciation of "Shaolin Temple Kung Fu") is officially recognized as a religious body. In Indonesia the martial art of silat is taught in conjunction with religious instruction. Catechism accompanies every stage of training, and silat styles are known by their association with either Christianity, Islam or the native animist religion.

George Dillman with Danny Pai and Ed Parker in 1967.

Many of the most famous martial artists of the last century have been devoutly religious. Morihei Ueshiba, the founder of Aikido, was a Shinto priest. Gogen "The Cat" Yamaguchi, the founder of the Japanese Goju-kai was also a priest. Shosei Kina, the last surviving student of the great kobudo (weapons) master Sanda Kanagusuku, was a devout Christian who lived into his 90's. The late martial arts master Danny Pai was a Pentecostal Christian and a bishop of his church. The late Ed Parker, founder of American Kenpo, was a devout Mormon. Kung fu expert Leo Fong is a retired Methodist minister.

With such strong religious inclinations, it is not surprising that the traditional martial arts have always contemplated the problem of morality in self-defense. In India, Buddhist martial artists are said to have taught deadly pressure point techniques (a largely lost art called marma adi, which is very similar to kyusho-jitsu) side by side with antidote techniques. In this way, they believed they could defend themselves, then immediately counter-act the effect so as to keep their vow to never take a life (Zarrilli, 1992). In China, the monks are said to have only used a staff as a weapon, and avoided spears or swords so that they could protect themselves without killing. And in Okinawa the most cherished principle of karate is "Karateni wa sente nashi," which loosely translates to, "Karate is for self-defense only."

Even so, many religious people have difficulty reconciling the concept of self-defense with the moral principles of universal love and treating others as you would want to be treated — principles common to religions around the world.

This can be especially true for Christians. Jesus of Nazareth said, "If someone strikes you on the cheek, turn to him the other, that he might strike it also." This teaching lies at the very heart of Christian ethics — namely, that suffering and sacrifice have redemptive power, the very ability to change people's lives. Jesus demonstrated this behavior by allowing himself to be arrested and crucified. And when his followers rose up to his defense and attacked his enemies, Jesus told them, "Put away your sword; for whoever lives by the sword shall die by the sword."

But, what many people who seek to follow Jesus' example fail to realize is that Jesus himself did not regard every attack to be a suitable occasion to "turn the other cheek." There are instances in the Gospels (Christian scripture which record the life and teaching of Jesus) when crowds of people sought to kill Jesus. Rather than turning the other cheek, Jesus defended himself using the most effective technique of all — he escaped (Luke 4:29-30, John 8:59, John 10:39).

The Gospels also record a time when Jesus acted violently. Upon entering the Temple in Jerusalem — the very heart of Jewish worship — he found that the entire operation had become a money-making enterprise. Outraged that faith had been replaced by commercialism, he grabbed a length of rope and, using it as a whip drove all of the vendors away, declaring, "It is written, My house shall be a house of prayer for all nations! But you have turned it into den of thieves."

Apparently, Jesus believed that there were circumstances when turning the other cheek was not an act of sacrificial love, but simply a wasted effort. As Jesus himself taught, "Do not cast your pearls before swine, and do not give what is holy to dogs. The swine will simply trample your pearls under foot, and the dogs will turn and tear you to pieces."

Perhaps the religious person's dilemma can be resolved simply by thinking of the self-defense problem problem differently. Consider this, If you come upon someone being attacked by another person, is it a loving act to protect the victim even with the use of force? In the same way, isn't it just as loving to protect the victim when you are the victim? If you allow yourself to be brutalized, aren't you giving what is holy (your own precious being) to the dogs?

And, one must also ask if it really shows love for an assailant to do nothing and thereby allow him to compound his sins? Doesn't it harm his soul to let him continue his violent behavior unopposed? Wouldn't stopping him be an act of kindness towards him? (An interesting note along those lines is this: Among some pressure point practitioners it is believed that an attacker must be sick, physically, emotionally or spiritually, or he wouldn't be acting violently. Using pressure points in self-defense is regarded as a form of therapeutic treatment for the attacker. The act of self-defense is an act of love, since it shows love for the victim by protecting him or her, and love for the assailant by treating his illness.)

One irony in this discussion is the fact that attackers do not wrestle with these moral issues, and in fact count on the morality of their intended victims, even to the point of using it against them. But, good and decent people must always engage in such moral and ethical thinking, and will always second-guess themselves and their motives if they ever find themselves using physical force in self-defense. Even *Humane Pressure Point Self-Defense* cannot completely resolve the inner conflict, though it is one of the most moral methods of self-protection to be found.

ANATOMY OF A STREET FIGHT

Street fights and barroom brawls are fairly common in places where young males congregate. These encounters usually follow a set pattern (Quinn, 1990). Understanding the anatomy of these encounters can be useful in spotting trouble before it starts, making it possible to predict impending violence.

1. Target Acquisition: Street fights do not "just happen." They occur because someone is looking for a fight, or, more accurately, someone is looking to beat someone else up. So, the perpetrator looks for a target, a person he thinks he can easily intimidate and defeat. It is not possible to know what criteria he is using in his selection process, but, a person watching you closely is an early clue of violence.

2. The Grievance: Since the goal is to beat someone else up, the perpetrator will seek to verify his selection of targets with an initial feint. Typically, this will take the form of some invented grievance. For example, he might intentionally bump into his target, and then proclaim, "Hey, watch where you're going." Another common strategy is to wait until the target happens to glance his way, then express offense with the words, "What are you looking at?" It should be noted that he will usually regard his grievance as genuine. This allows him to feel justified, and even vindicated, by his own violent behavior (overcoming what is called *cognitive dissonance*). Remember, no perpetrator really believes that he is a "bad" person. A person suddenly taking offense at you is a warning sign.

3. Posturing: Since the instigator of a street fight is usually a bully (see above) he operates by the "Intimidate then perpetrate" rule. So, before moving to physical confrontation he will "posture." This involves dramatic gestures, loud aggressive speech, rolling up his sleeves, punching into his palm, and similar threatening displays. This behavior is primarily to frighten and intimidate the intended target. It also bolsters his own courage before he commits himself to a fight that he is still not sure he will win.

　　At this point in the encounter, the most effective self-defense response is to be calm, composed and ready to fight. Your readiness to fight must be entirely an inward commitment. Do not take a fighting stance or appear as if you are accepting a challenge, though a Non-confrontational Ready Position (see page 165) is appropriate. Do not engage in posturing yourself, as this can force the fight by involving pride and ego. You may apologize for the "slight" which he has made into his grievance and offer to buy him a beer. This gives him an "out" if he feels he must prove something to his friends, and, more importantly, it undermines his ability to paint himself as the "injured party," robbing him of the "right" to act violently. If these efforts work and he walks away, your best course of action is to leave, since he may return to try again.

4. The Push & Punch: From the above step, one of two outcomes will follow if the situation continues to escalate towards violence. The first of these is the push and punch. Typically, after sufficient posturing — and especially if the target postures in return — the perpetrator will push or shove the target. Usually, the target stiffens up to resist the push, and then shoves back. A brief pushing match ensues which will quickly turn into flying fists. The punching generally occurs in the following manner: each combatant (at this point, there is no longer a perpetrator and a target, just a couple of idiots swinging at each other) will grab the other's shirt at the right shoulder with his left hand, while trying to hit to the head with his right fist. A common result is that the shirts will be torn. Individuals who seek out this kind of confrontation may actually remove their shirts ahead of time. If you see an individual take off his shirt, it is a sign that he is getting ready for the push and punch fight.

5. The Look-Away & Sucker-Punch: If the situation does not become a push and punch, then it will probably become a look-away and sucker-punch. At some point during the posturing phase, either the perpetrator or the target will look away. Sometimes the target will look away because he is looking for help, or responding to something someone else says. Sometimes he will look away because he is afraid and intimidated. When the perpetrator sees the target look away, he will throw the sucker-punch. If the target does not look away, then the perpetrator will. He will turn as if to leave, sometimes taking a few steps, then without warning, spin back and throw the punch. It is very important that you do not look away from an aggressor during the posturing phase, unless you are at least nine feet away from him. Then, only look away for a split second to scan for other attackers or hazards. If you are closer than nine feet, do not look away for any reason. If you see the aggressor look away from you, assume that he will attack. Take a step back, or a step forward and to the side. Then, if he does attack, you will not be where he expects you to be.

6. To The Ground: As the combatants start throwing punches and grabbing at each other, they will very often end up on the ground wrestling. If this happens, expect that within 30 seconds someone will interfere. Sometimes this comes in the form of bystanders trying to pull the combatants apart (many a person has been injured at this point in the fight, because people were holding his arms and pulling him off the other man, who took that opportunity to hit or kick). Very often, a friend of one of the two will join the fray by kicking his buddy's adversary in the head. This is a situation with potentially life-threatening consequences. Most people with experience in street fights know this instinctively, and will quickly break away and scramble to their feet if the confrontation goes to the ground. However, people with experience in grappling arts (wrestlers or Jujitsu players) will sometimes forget this, since their training has made them very comfortable on the ground. Feeling confident that they will win, they forget about the interference of others at great risk to themselves.

"The non-violent restraint techniques are practical and effective during apprehension and personal defense situations."

Jeff Brown
Loss Prevention Manager
Detroit Michigan

CHAPTER TWO: Creating Advantage

The people who need self-defense knowledge are not generally able to rely on brute force and strength. The fact that they are being assaulted implies that the attacker is bigger and stronger, or enjoys some other strategic advantage. Therefore, the methods of self-defense cannot rely on strength, but on principles which nullify the advantage of the attacker, and create advantage for the defender.

Fortunately, every individual, no matter how physically imposing, has natural vulnerabilities. The secret to successful self-defense is capitalizing on these inherent weaknesses. The central method of *Humane Pressure Point Self-Defense* is the use of pressure points. These are covered in detail in the next chapter. In this chapter, we will reveal additional human weaknesses and how to exploit them.

The essence to effective self-defense can be summed up in this way, "Direct your strength against your assailant's weakness." For example, if you are attacked by a powerful body-builder, his arms will be much stronger than your arms. However, your arm is still much stronger than his little finger. So if you pit your strength against him, move for move, you will lose. But, if you direct all your might against just one of his fingers, he will lose.

All of the physical movements which we employ in *Humane Pressure Point Self-Defense* are based on this principle. In every case, we assume that the attacker has superior strength. So, we design our self-defense solutions to avoid his strength and exploit his weakness. In the following pages we will illustrate and explain some important principles about exploiting weakness through the use of specific examples.

THE DIRECTION OF STRENGTH:
Adduction vs. Abduction

It is frequently taught that, when an assailant grabs for you with both hands, you should bring your hands up between his, and knock them outward. However, this does not work. Try the following test with a partner and you will understand.

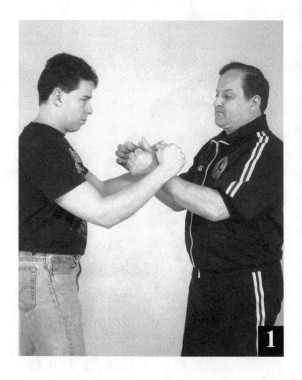

1. Your partner stands with both arms in front. You bring both of your hands up between his.

2. Try to push your arms outward with all your strength, while your partner holds his arms in position.

Your greatest strength is found when your hands are close to the base of your sternum. This means that movements inward, toward your center, are physically stronger than movements outward, away from the center. To put it in terms of physiology, adduction (movement towards the center) is more powerful than abduction (movement outward) because the muscles of the chest which are used in adduction are stronger than the muscles of the back which are used in abduction.

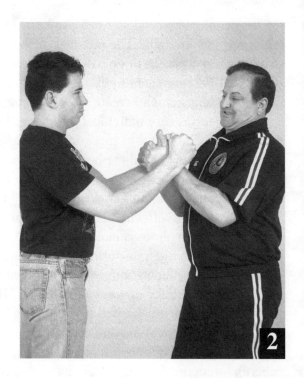

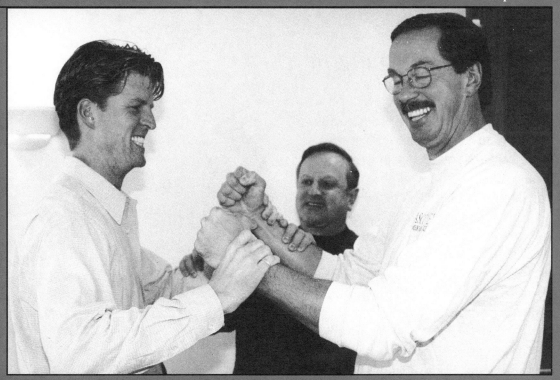

Martial artists and non-martial artists alike train in Dillman Method. Non-martial artists appreciate the simple concepts, effective approach and humane techniques. Martial artists find that Dillman Method unlocks the secrets of the traditional arts.

THE DIRECTION OF STRENGTH (Cont.)

In the preceding exercise, you are unable to drive your partner's arms outward because you are pushing away from your strength, while he is squeezing into his strength. This means that you are directing your weakness against his strength, giving him the advantage.

1. Try the exercise again. This time your partner tries to hold his position while you squeeze inward.

2-3. You can easily cross his arms, because you are pitting your strength against his weakness.

4. Once his arms are crossed, you have created a tactical advantage because you can now control both of his hands with one of yours. You will have one or two seconds to attack with your free hand while his hands are tied up.

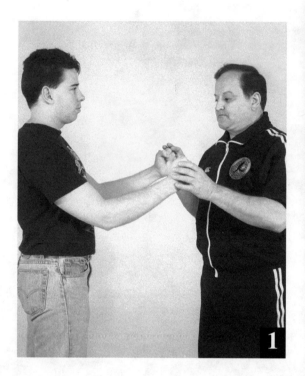

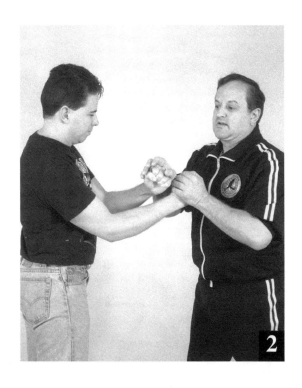

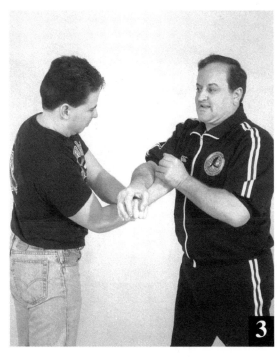

POSITIONING FOR STRENGTH:
Controlling from the Outside

If a person is strongest performing inward motions, it follows that in self-defense you would not want to stand between an assailant's arms. Instead, you should seek to position yourself outside one of his arms. When you do this, you are able to use both of your arms to control one of his arms, while you have placed yourself out of reach of his other arm.

1. One of the simplest ways to accomplish this is by footwork. If an attacker reaches for you with one hand, step forward and to his outside.

2-3. You can also work to the outside by using the arm crossing principle we have discussed. When an assailant reaches with both hands, begin by crossing his arms.

4. In our example, you have crossed his his right arm over his left. Therefore, grab his right wrist with your right hand. At this moment, his left hand is stuck underneath his right arm. You control both of his arms with one hand.

5-6. Pivot to his right and pull his right hand towards your hip. With your left hand strike the Triceps Hit Point (see page 80) causing him to fold over.

NOTE: You are using both of your arms to attack one of his arms, and you have gained control from the outside.

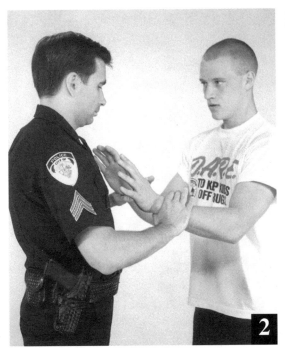
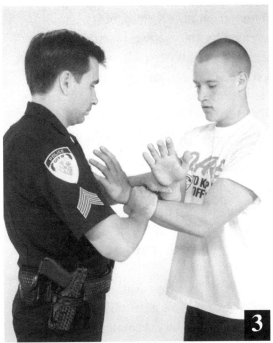

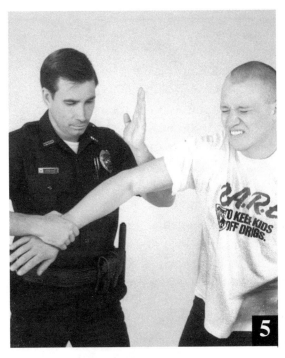
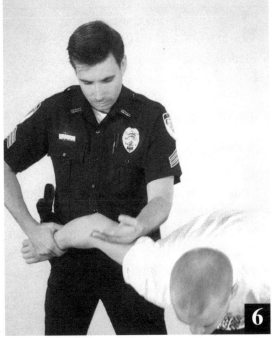

CREATING IMBALANCE

There is another vulnerability which is created by the method of crossing the arms. When a person's arms are crossed in the manner we have shown, he is temporarily off-balance. Once you have crossed someone's arms, it is easy to push them away or pull them forward.

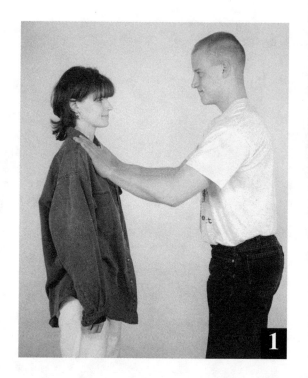

1-3. When an assailant lays his hands on you, you do not try to knock his arms away. Instead, you slam his arms inward so that they are crossed.

4-5. With his arms crossed he becomes unbalanced. You must take advantage of this momentary weakness by immediately pushing forward with both hands, driving his crossed arms into his chest, and knocking him backwards.

This is an excellent technique to use preemptively as well. Remember that an attacker will usually probe at you using some form of verbal or physical intimidation. This is designed to cause indecision and inaction on your part. If your body starts to pump out adrenaline, but you do not move, you become paralyzed and unable to act. The moment you feel any threat or discomfort, the moment your body starts to react with the "fight or flight" response, you must take some action.

If you simply push the attacker's arms across his chest (and the good news is that you only need to cross one of his arms over his body to produce the desired result) then drive him away with a good hard shove, you can make a hasty escape. In the process you have stopped his aggression cold. But, your preemptive move was not a punch or blow. You have protected yourself, taken an immediate positive action (and thereby set yourself into action mode instead of indecisive mode), and created an opportunity for you to escape (always the second best defense, after avoidance), while minimizing the risk that you would be charged with assault or accused of "starting it."

To use a "preemptive" technique such as this one, you must be willing to be insulted by the assailant in response to your actions. Caring about the good opinion of a complete stranger is a great hindrance to self-defense. You have the right to say "No." You have the right to be left alone. You have the right to rebuff the unwanted approach of another. You have the right to defend yourself.

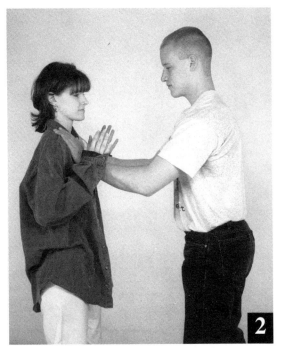

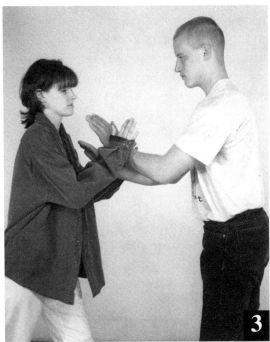

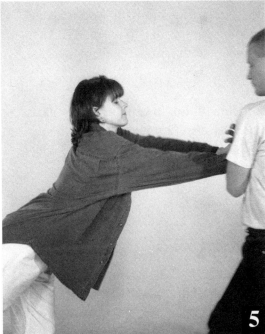

CONTROLLING THE FINGER

As we have mentioned, your arm is stronger than one of an assailant's fingers. So, manipulating the finger is an effective means of controlling a self-defense situation.

1. When controlling a finger, catch it in the "V" between your thumb and index finger.

2-3. Do not think of bending the finger back. Instead, pull the base of the assailant's finger towards you. If you do this, the tip of the finger will move one way and the base another. This is called "Small-Circle Theory" and was developed by the great jujitsu master Wally Jay.

4. Draw the finger in close to your body, into your strength. You may also lock his palm against your body. Then as you bend his finger, he cannot escape.

5-6. In addition to bending his finger, you may also turn it so that the palm of his hand faces upward. This will enable you to bring him up onto his toes. Use your free hand to apply counter-pressure against his wrist. In this way, his finger is trapped between your two hands, and you can control the level of pain you inflict.

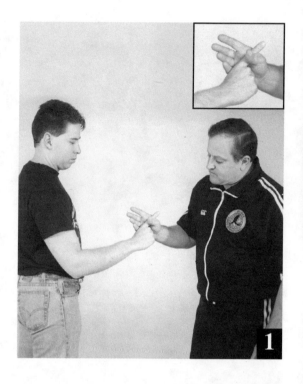

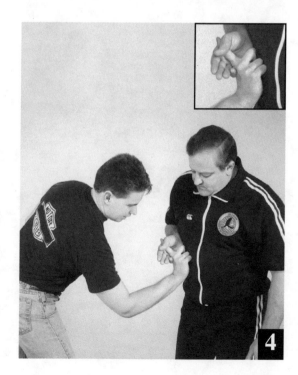

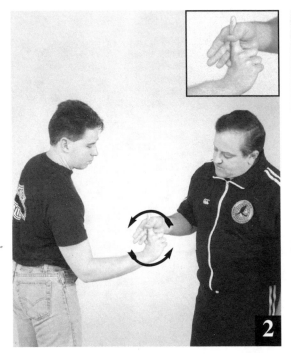

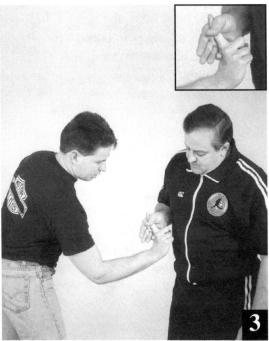

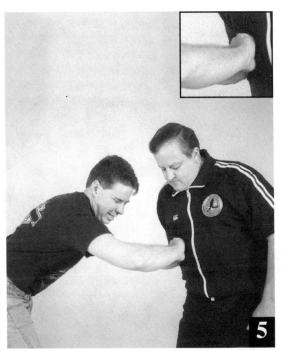

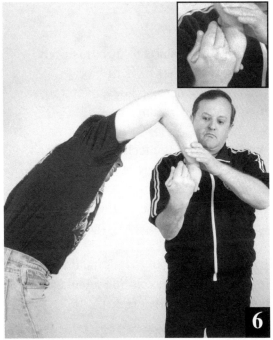

HEAD TURNING: Using the Hair

"Where the head goes, the body follows." This saying is important for
self-defense because you can move an
attacker with relative ease by controlling his head.

1. Begin by reaching around your
attacker's head with your <u>left hand and
firmly grasp his hair on the left rear
portion of his scalp.</u> At the same time,
lay the edge of your right hand along
the right side of his face.

*NOTE: Be careful to grasp well past
the center-line of the head on the left
rear quadrant.*

2-4. Using a two-way motion, turn his
head to your right (his left) by pulling
with your left hand and pushing with
your right.

Once his head starts to turn, his body
will follow. After he is in motion, you
can control where he goes, even throwing him to the ground.

A. To perform the technique on the
other side, simply grasp his hair on the
right rear portion of his scalp with your
right hand, and press on the left side of
his face with the edge of your left hand.

B. Pulling with your right hand pushing with your left, spin the attacker's
head to your left (his right).

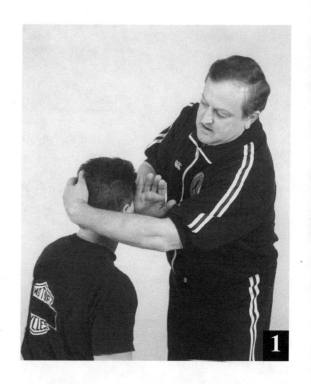

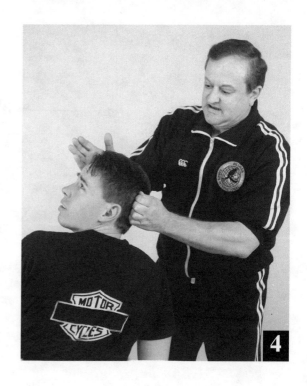

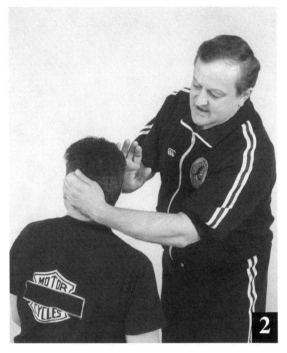
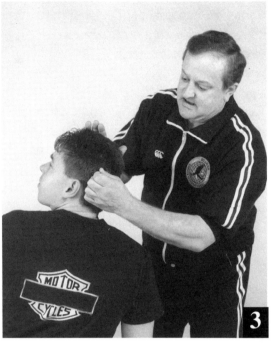
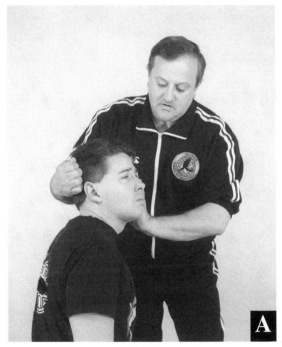
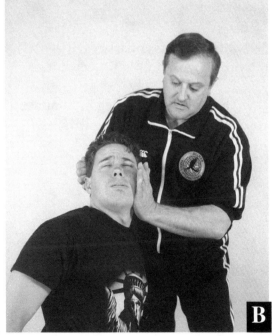

HEAD TURNING: Using the Ear

Sometimes an attacker does not have enough hair to grab on to. In those cases, simply use his ear to control his head.

A. Pulling the ear away from the head is not very effective, because there are not many nerves at the juncture of the ear and the scalp.

B. However, a branch of the auriculo-temporal nerve passes into the ear at about the point where the apex of the ear connects to the head. When the ear is twisted back and down, the nerve is stretched causing pain. The head will move to escape the pain.

1. To control someone's head using the ear, grasp the ear as if to form your fist around it.

2. Next twist the ear back and down as if trying to twist it from the head.

3-4. Once the assailant begins to move, you can direct his body at will.

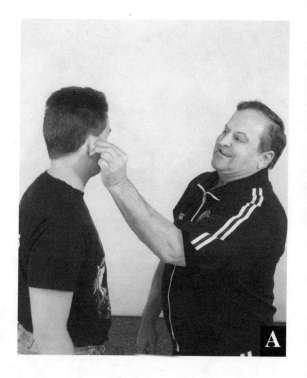

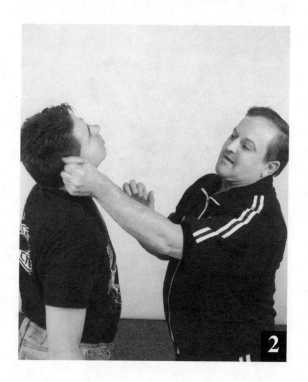

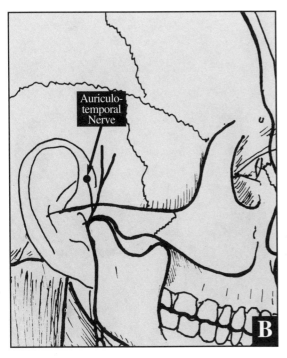

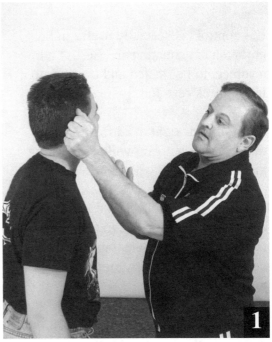

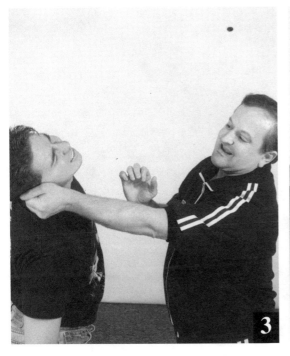

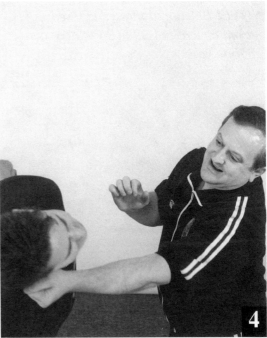

HEAD TURNING: Using the Ear (Cont.)

Ear control is especially useful in law enforcement situations because it allows a subject to be rotated and drawn into a lateral neck restraint.

1. With your right hand firmly grasp the subject's left ear, while controlling his right shoulder with your left hand.

2-3. Twist his ear back and turn inward, causing his head to turn to the right (his left). At the same time, push his shoulder down and towards your right to spin him around.

4. As the subject turns, he will turn into the crook of your arm, virtually placing himself into a lateral neck restraint.

NOTE: Be careful that your forearm is tucked beneath his chin so that he cannot bite you.

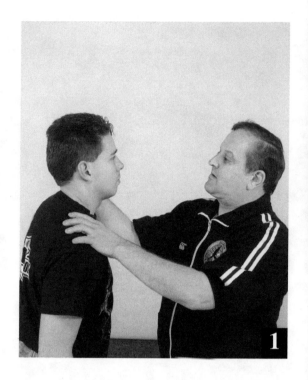

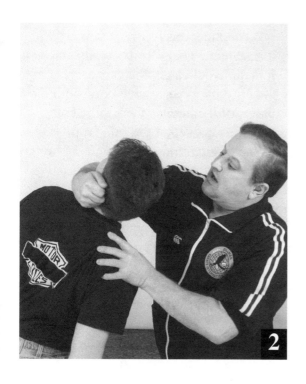

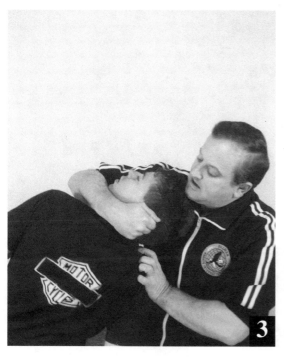

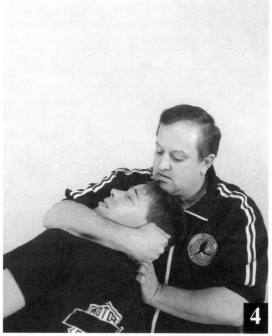

VITAL TARGETS

The pressure points which we discuss in the next chapter are unexpected areas of vulnerability. It is as if the body doesn't realize these points exist. Vital targets, on the other hand, are the areas of weakness that everyone knows and protects.

Attacks to vital targets can be very effective. For this reason it is important to be familiar with them and ready at any time to attack them. Attacks to vital targets are only occasionally applied in *Humane Pressure Point Self-Defense*. This is because attacks to vital targets are generally intended to cause injury. Sometimes, though, an attack to a vital target is done to produce a predictable reaction from an attacker (for example, a strike to the eyes will cause someone to blink). Vital targets can also be used in conjunction with pressure points.

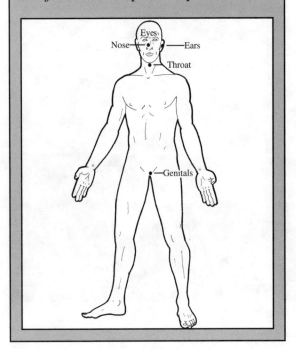

ATTACKING THE EARDRUM

The inner-ear is a very sensitive instrument. That sensitivity also means it is quite delicate. The ears are attacked by a concussive blow with the palms of the hands. Generally, both ears are attacked at the same time, using a clapping motion of the hands. The attack must not be delicate or tentative, but delivered with full force.

1. An attacker is very close and is encircling you with his arms.

2-3. Slap both ears with the cupped palms of your hands, then escape.

CAUTION: *A strong cuff to the ear can cause permanent hearing loss.*

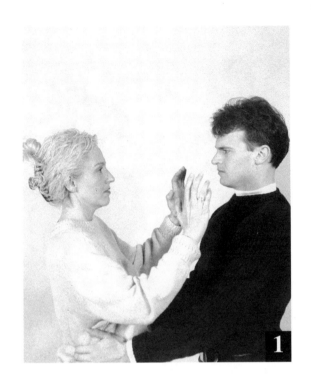

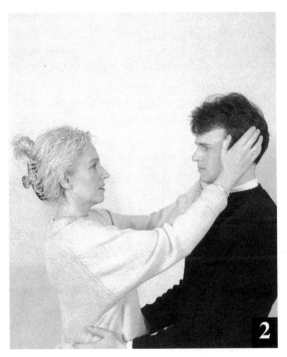

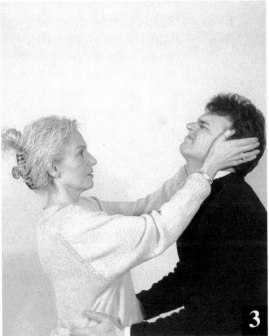

ATTACKING THE EYES

Straight, jabbing attacks with the tips of the fingers are the best method of striking the eyes [A]. Generally speaking, a quick finger-tip jab will not cause permanent damage. This is because the eye is the fastest healing organ of the body. The eye is also pro-tected by tremendous reflexes. The eyelid and the muscles around the eye provide an effective barrier against injury. However, always attack the eyes with the intent to injure, otherwise your technique will be slow and ineffective.

One of the best ways to seriously injure the eyes, is to use your thumb to gouge into the eye-socket [B,C].

1. An attacker has moved close to you. You raise your hands toward his face in a non-threatening manner.

2-3. Slide your right hand behind his head, then grab his hair to hold him in place while you jam your thumb into his eye socket.

NOTE: Serious attacks to the eyes can result in changes in heart rhythm. This is known as the "oculocardiac reflex." Stretch receptors located in the eye muscles (particularly the medial rectus) respond to pressure on the eye by send-ing a nerve signal which can result in a profound slowing of the heart (reflex bradycardia) and even arrest (asystole).

The eye can also be used to create vulnerability in several of the pressure points discussed in the next chapter.

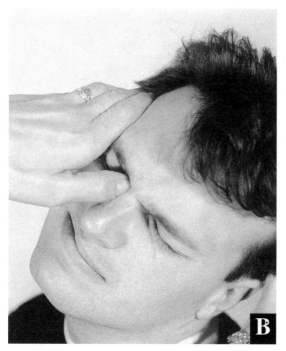

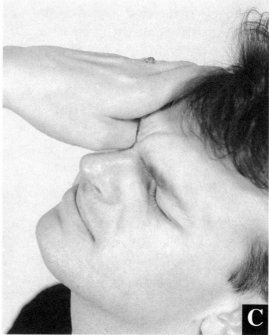

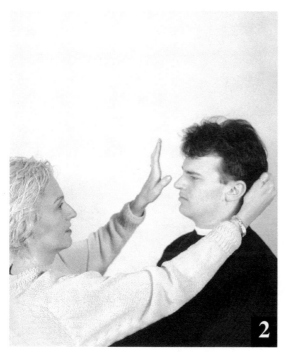

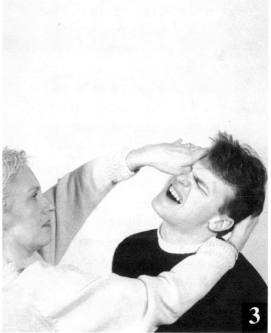

ATTACKING THE NOSE

Attacks to the nose are not deadly, despite myths about driving the nasal bone into the brain. The fact of the matter is that the nose is attacked primarily to produce two predictable effects: First, the nose bleeds easily. A strike to the nose can draw blood and at the sight of his own blood, many an attacker will lose his nerve. Second, a blow to the nose can cause the eyes to tear up, making it difficult for an assailant to see. An attacker who cannot see clearly is easier to escape from.

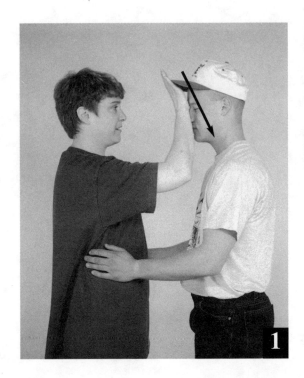

The most effective strike against the nose is a downward blow [1]. This attack is aimed at the juncture of the nasal bone and the nasal cartilage. The body interprets a downward blow as if the cartilage is being pulled away from the bone. This stretches and irritates the anterior ethmoidal nerve (also called the external nasal branch of the ophthalmic nerve) [A]. In addition to the pain this causes, it also disrupts vision.

A second and very effective means of striking the nose is to hit it from the side, at about the place the nose pads of eye-glasses rest [2]. This particularly causes the eyes to tear up. It also puts the pressure of the impact along the nasomaxillary suture, a weakness in the bone structure [B]. Blows to the side of the nose can cause the nose to break, resulting in some disfigurement of the face (which can usually be repaired).

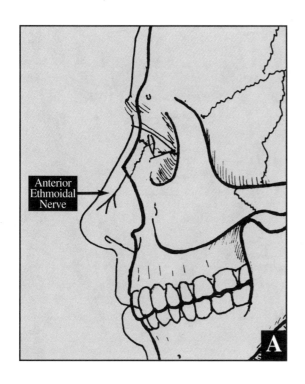

Anterior Ethmoidal Nerve

A

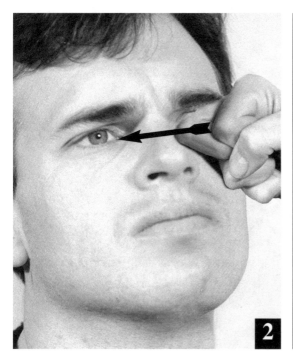

2

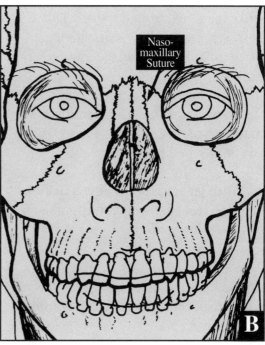

Naso-maxillary Suture

B

ATTACKING THE THROAT

Attacks to the throat are potentially life threatening. The esophagus itself can be easily crushed. The resulting collapse and swelling of the wind-pipe can cause suffocation unless the airway is restored. A non-lethal blow can cause an attacker to be incapacitated by a fit of gasping and choking.

There are two directions of attack which are the most effective. The first is to strike diagonally upward, hitting between the bulge of the Adam's apple and the base of the neck (one third the distance from the Supra-Sternal [Jugular] notch to the Adam's apple) [A]. This is even more effective if the attacker's head is tipped back first. This blow is usually executed with the extended knuckle of a single finger [B].

The second method of attack is to strike the throat from the side. This blow is typically delivered with the extended knuckle of the middle finger [C].

It is essential to stress again that such blows can kill. This consideration must be a part of any decision to strike an attacker in the throat.

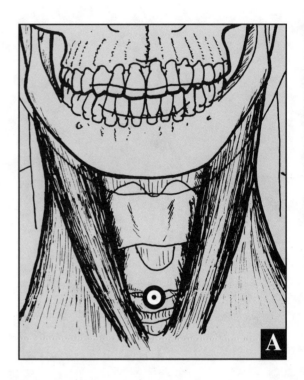

1. When an attacker grabs you in close quarters, reach up with your right hand and grasp his hair.

2-3. Pull his head back to stretch and expose his wind-pipe, and strike upward with the extended knuckle of your middle finger.

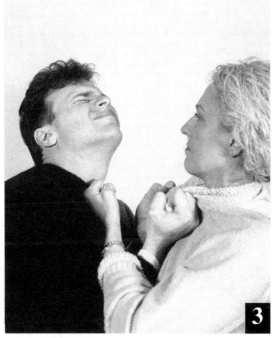

ATTACKING THE GENITALS

Men are very good at protecting their testicles, therefore, the secret to attacking this target is to get very close. A rising blow with the knee, shin or foot can be effective if the testicles are held firmly against the pelvic bone by clothing. Because this is uncertain, it is recommended that upward blows to this vital target be repeated two or three times. If your assailant tries to protect his groin by covering it with his hands, just kick his hands.

1. An assailant places his right hand on your shoulder menacingly.

2. With your left hand, pull down and inward on his arm at his elbow, as you lift your knee towards his groin.

3. As he pulls his groin away, extend your leg and kick him in the genitals with your shin.

NOTE: As the assailant pulls his groin away, he actually exposes the Inner Thigh Point (Sp-10, see page 90). A better strategy is to kick this pressure point, instead of kicking to the groin.

4-5. When the assailant covers his groin with his hands, simply kick him again in his hands.

ATTACKING THE GENITALS
(Cont.)

A more effective and unexpected means of attacking the testicles is to strike downward. A downward blow pulls the testicles away from the body, stretching the nerves and producing immediate pain. Punching downward at about a 30 to 45 degree angle will be an almost unstoppable blow when delivered at close range.

1-2. As an assailant reaches for you, do not pull away, but draw your right hand back, ready to punch. *(This action actually draws the attacker in closer as he tries to reach around you.)*

3-4. Punch downward into the attacker's groin as you sink your weight forward.

NOTE: As you punch to the groin with your right hand, move your head slightly to the left. This is to prevent the attacker's head from hitting yours as he buckles over.

A. Directly beside the groin are the Inguinal Crease Points (Li-12 & Sp-12, see page 88). If your punch is off target, you will hit the pressure point instead of the genitals. Since this is also highly effective, this defense solution is very practical, having a built in margin of error.

If the nature of an assault is sexual violence, and your attacker has exposed his genitals, grab his testicles with one or both hands. Squeeze your hands into tight fists so that the tips of your fingers press inward. At the same time, pull and twist as hard as you can.

"Dillman's system is the most humane and easy method of control and survival for anyone, especially women and police officers."

Phil Harris
Former Police Detective
Denver, CO

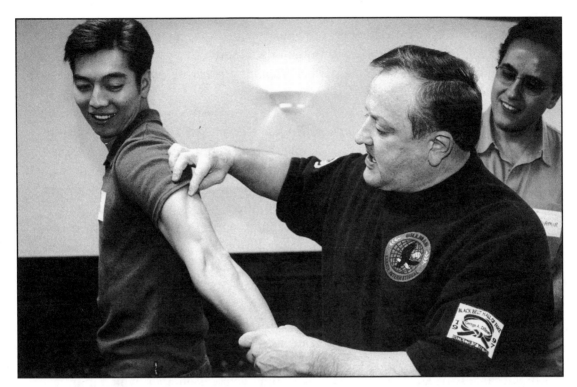

CHAPTER THREE: The Pressure Points

Humane Pressure Point Self-Defense depends upon the use of pressure points— the same points used in acupuncture and *shiatsu*. These are places on the body that, when properly stimulated, produce a predictable outcome. Pressure points are more useful than vital targets in two ways. First, pressure points are largely ignored by the body's natural defenses. Consider the eyes. A poke to the eyes would be very effective. However, the body is so conditioned to protect the eyes that any movement towards them causes a protective blink. A kick to the groin will elicit a similar response. Men are so accustomed to protecting themselves in this area, that the slightest threat produces an immediate protective action. Pressure points, however, are not a part of this protective system. One would never think of the inside of the arm as a place vulnerable to attack. So, the reflex to protect is not ingrained.

Second, pressure points are superior to vital targets because pressure point attacks are less likely to cause serious injury; therefore, they are more humane. Pressure points work by disrupting the energy of the body and tricking the nerves. It might be compared with a brief power outage during a thunderstorm. The lights go out then come back on; your computer shuts down then reboots itself. Nothing is harmed.

This does not mean that pressure point fighting is not dangerous. In fact, *Humane Pressure Point Self-Defense* is based on the quite lethal art of kyusho-jitsu — sometimes called "the death touch." But, the methods presented here are designed to produce the maximum results with the minimum risk of injury to you or your assailant.

However, you must constantly bear in mind that there is always the risk of serious injury in any physical confrontation. Obviously you, as the intended victim, are in danger of being harmed. If you do nothing, or act ineffectively, you will almost certainly be injured. Even if you do a perfect *Humane Pressure Point Self-Defense* technique, you could still be injured.

On the other hand, your assailant could be injured despite your desire to cause no harm. Even if you do a perfect *Humane Pressure Point Self-Defense* technique, he could still be hurt accidentally. For example, he might fall and strike his head on a piece of furniture. So, we must repeat this paradox again: you cannot defend yourself humanely unless you are willing to cause harm to your assailant. Despite your best efforts, you and/or your assailant may well be injured in the course of an assault.

Pressure points are interconnected. These interconnections defy analysis by conventional medicine, but they are described in traditional Chinese medicine (acupuncture). This interconnection may be compared to the familiar game of "paper-scissors-rock." In this game, you and a friend show either an open hand (paper), two fingers (scissors) or a fist (rock). If you show "paper", and your friend shows "rock", you win, because, "Paper covers rock." But, if your friend shows "scissors", you lose, because, "Scissors cut paper." And, if your friend had "scissors", but you chose "rock", you would be the winner. "Rock smashes scissors."

In the same way, attacking one pressure point weakens another, which in turn weakens another. The self-defense solutions presented in this book take these relationships into account. We will mention some of these relationships as we describe the points, but it is better to learn them by actually practicing the moves we show later.

There are three things which you must know if you are going to use pressure points properly.

> •**You must know exactly where each point is.**
> Locate them on yourself first, then practice finding them on other people.
> •**You must know what mode of stimulation is required for each point.**
> Some points respond to touch, some to rubbing, and others to striking.
> •**You must know the correct direction of activation.**
> Each pressure point has a unique angle of attack.

In the following pages, a number of pressure points are carefully described for you. Location, mode of activation, angle of attack, as well as methods of weakening each point are given. Study this material carefully. Also, you will note that the points are given simple descriptive names (such as "Lower Wrist Point"). But, there is also an organ and number associated with each point (Heart # 6, H-6). This is the identification of the point used in acupuncture and is provided as a matter of reference.

POINT NAME: Hand Energy Points
(Heart # 8/H-8 &
Triple Warmer # 3/TW-3)

LOCATION: H-8 is on the palm where the tip of the little finger touches when the hand is formed into a loose fist [1]. TW-3 is on the back of the hand between and just below the knuckles of the fourth and fifth fingers [2]. These points lie directly opposite each other.

METHOD: With the Energy Points touching, visualize your energy, like flowing water, passing from the palm of one hand into the back of the other. Men should place their right fist into their left palm as shown [A], women should place left into right. These points are used for controlling your own energy and strength for your protection.

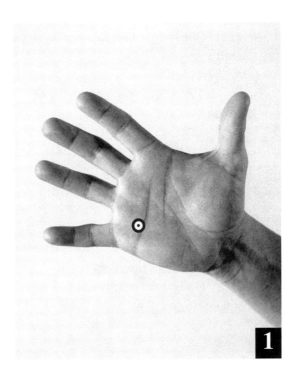

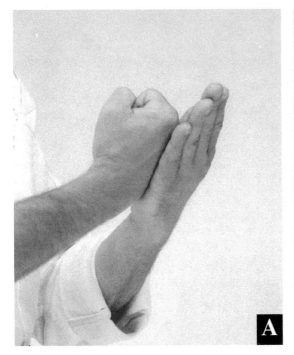

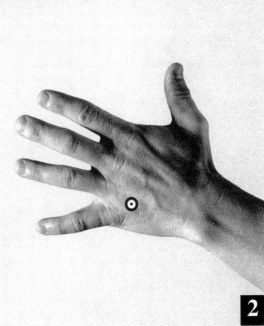

Hand Energy Points (Cont.)

1. An aggressor has placed his hands menacingly on your neck.

2. Bring your hands up on both sides of his left arm.

3. Touch your Hand Energy Points (H-8 & TW-3) – left fist in right palm – and picture energy flowing like water from your palm into your fist.

4. Jerk your linked hands sharply into your own strength so that they hit through the Outer Forearm Point (LI-10, see page 76) on your assailant's left arm.

5-6. Continue your movement by stepping back with your left foot, turning to your left and dropping your weight to propel him to the ground.

NOTE: Here we illustrate the women's method. Men should reverse this technique right to left. This is a result of the yin/yang differences of men and women.

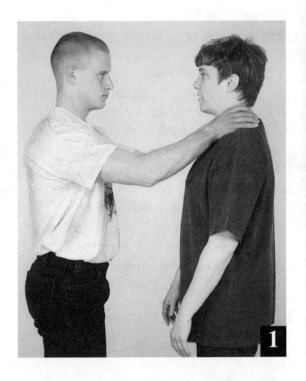

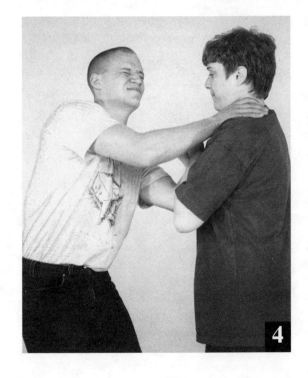

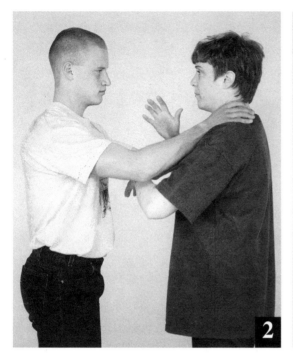

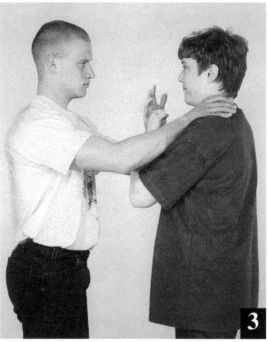

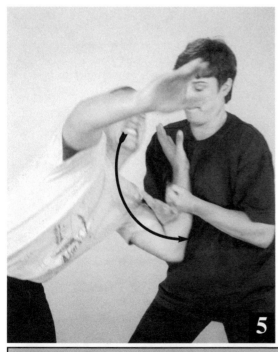

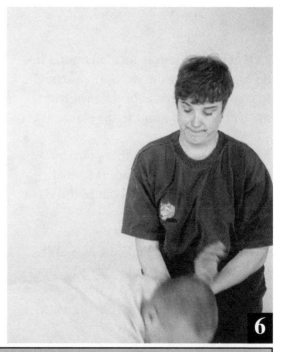

HINT: Once your assailant starts to move as a result of your strike to his Outer Forearm Point (LI-10), keep him moving by applying weight to his arm. If necessary, drop all the way down into a kneeling posture. The key is to learn the timing between step # 4 and steps 5-6.

POINT NAME: Upper Wrist Point
(Lung # 8/L-8)

LOCATION: L-8 is located 1/2 inch up from the crease of the wrist (towards the elbow) on the inside of the arm. It is where a nurse takes a pulse [1].

METHOD: Stimulate this point by rubbing it in the direction of the fist. A back and forth rubbing motion is a very effective method of accomplishing this. Properly stimulating this point will cause the hand to open up and the wrist to buckle [2,3].

VULNERABILITY: The Upper Wrist Point can be weakened by first stimulating the Lower Wrist Point (H-6, below).

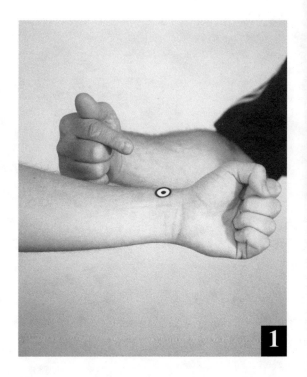

POINT NAME: Lower Wrist Point
(Heart # 6/H-6)

LOCATION: H-6 is located on the little finger side of the wrist, on a straight line across the inside of the arm from the Upper Wrist Point (L-8) [4].

METHOD: Stimulate this point by pressing it laterally across the wrist. Attacking this point will cause the wrist to bend [5,6].

VULNERABILITY: The Lower Wrist Point is made more vulnerable by first attacking the Lower Leg Point (Sp-6, see page 90), especially if you kick to the opposite leg.

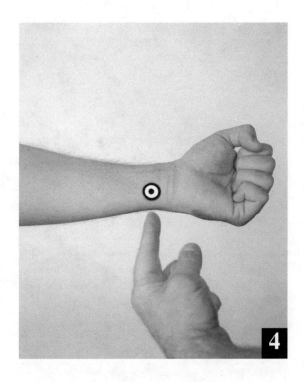

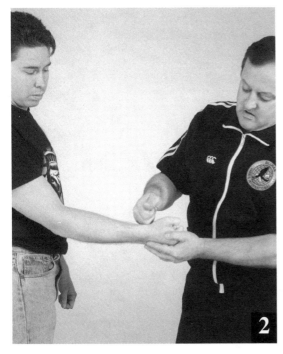

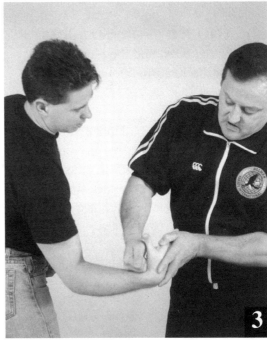

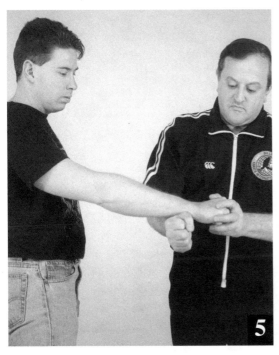

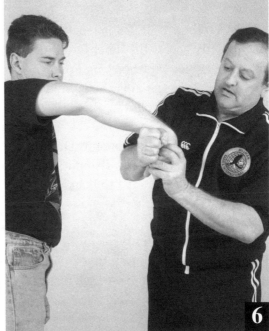

POINT NAME: Upper Mid-Forearm Point (Lung # 6/L-6)

LOCATION: L-6 is located halfway between the wrist and the elbow on the inside of the forearm, along the radial bone [1].

METHOD: Strike the Upper Mid-Forearm Point in a cutting motion towards the hand. This will cause the hand to open up and produce tingly sensations in the thumb and index fingers [2,3].

VULNERABILITY: This point can be weakened by attacking the Lower Wrist Point (H-6).

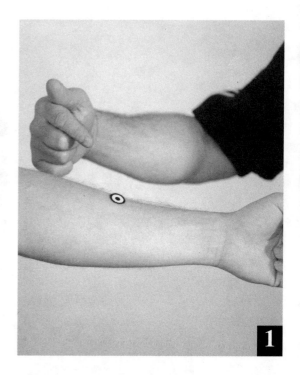

POINT NAME: Mid-Forearm Disarm Point (M-UE-28)

LOCATION: M-UE-28 is located on a line directly across the inner forearm from the Upper Mid-Forearm Point (L-6). It lies along the ulnar bone, midway between wrist and elbow [4].

METHOD: The Mid-Forearm Disarm Point must be struck in a rising motion. This will cause the wrist to buckle and the elbow to release [5,6].

VULNERABILITY: Weaken the Mid-Forearm Disarm Point by first attacking the Lower Leg Point (Sp-6, see page 90).

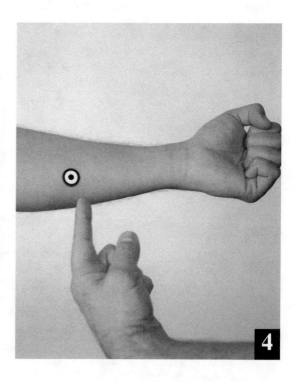

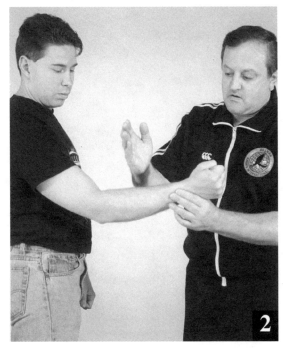

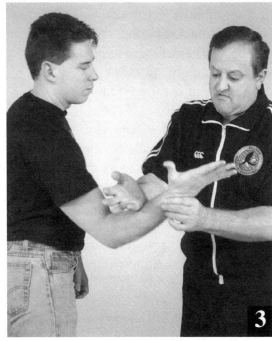

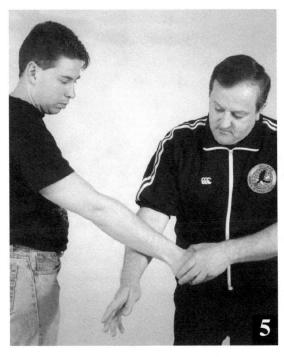

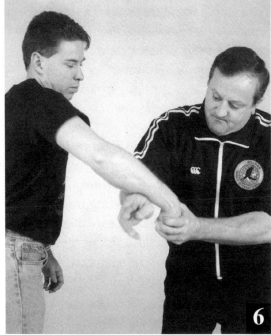

Mid-Forearm Disarm Point (Cont.)

1. The defender has grabbed a knife-wielding attacker by the wrist with his left hand. The defender turns the attacker's arm slightly inward to expose the Mid-Forearm Disarm Point.

2-3. Using his forearm in a stiff swinging motion the defender strikes the Mid-forearm Disarm Point at an upward angle.

4-5. The blow to the pressure point causes the attacker to drop the knife (which falls straight down), releases his elbow, and bends him over.

NOTE: One of the significant problems in disarming techniques is controlling where the attacker's weapon will fall. Since several of the points already discussed will make the hand open up, it would seem reasonable that any of them could be used to cause an attacker to drop a weapon. However, when other points are used for this purpose, the weapon is launched from the attacker's hand towards the defender's body. But, when the Mid-Forearm Disarm Point is used, the weapon drops straight down, or even back towards the attacker [6].

It should also be noted that when other points are used to release a gun, they can actually cause the subject to fire the weapon before release.

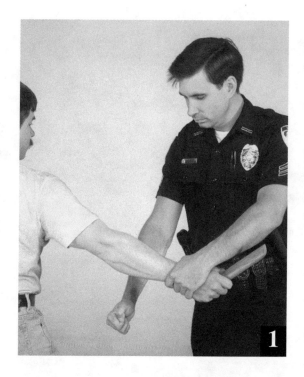

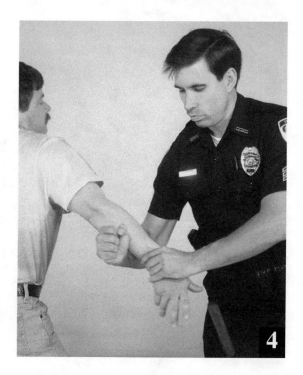

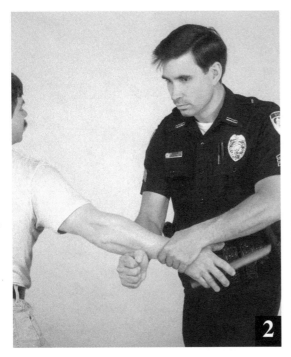

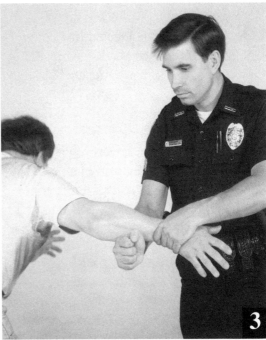

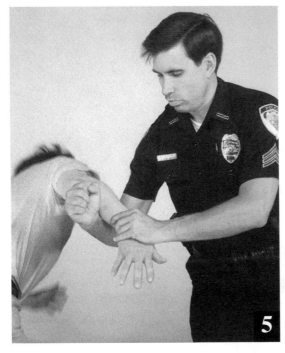

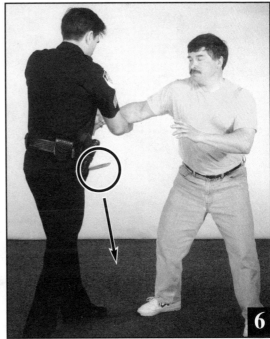

POINT NAME: Elbow Crease Point
(Lung # 5/L-5)

LOCATION: L-5 is located just below
the crease of the elbow, and just inside
the bulge of the forearm muscle [1].

METHOD: Strike this point with a
curving or cutting motion in which your
hand arcs back towards your own body.
When struck, the point will buckle the
knees, drop the head and shoulder forward, and cause the opposite arm to
swing away [2-5].

VULNERABILITY: The Elbow
Crease Point is weakened by grabbing
the Upper and Lower Wrist Points (L-8
& H-6) as shown. This point is also
made weak by the use of marijuana.

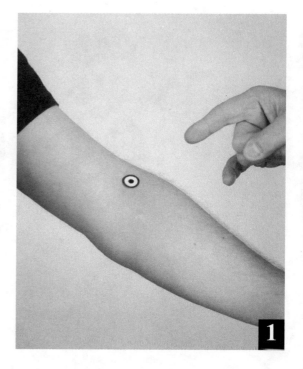

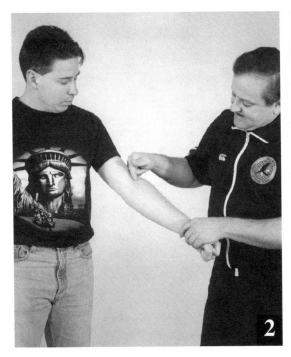

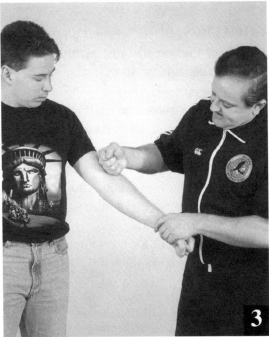

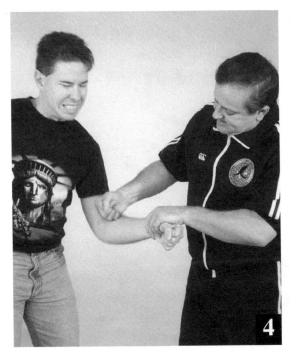

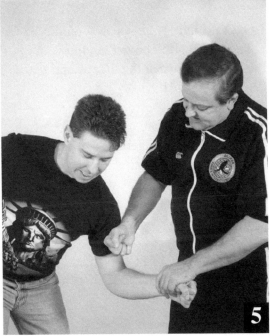

POINT NAME: Outer Forearm Point
(Large Intestine # 10/LI-10)

LOCATION: LI-10 is found on the
outside of the forearm just behind the
bulge of the forearm muscle [1].

METHOD: Strike or press this point
inward towards the body center to cause
the attacker's legs to give way and his
body to fold [2,3]. A blow to this point
can cause the arm to cramp and become
numb for up to twenty minutes.

VULNERABILITY: The Outer
Forearm Point is weakened by grabbing
the Upper and Lower Wrist Points (L-8
& H-6).

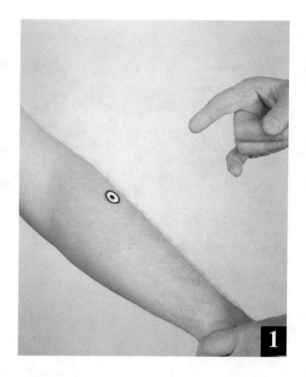

POINT NAME: Inner Arm Point
(Heart # 2/H-2)

LOCATION: H-2 is located on the
inside of the arm above the elbow, in
the hollow between the biceps and triceps muscles [4].

METHOD: A strike to this point causes
numbness in the fingertips and forces
the elbow to swing outward. Pressure
on this point causes an attacker to rise
up on his toes and raise his shoulders
[5,6].

VULNERABILITY: The Inner Arm
Point is weakened by touching the
Lower Wrist Point (H-6).

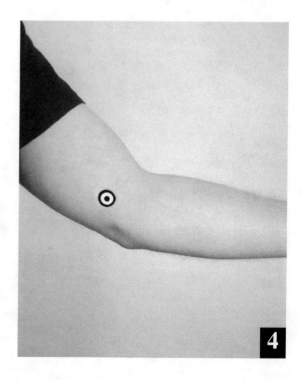

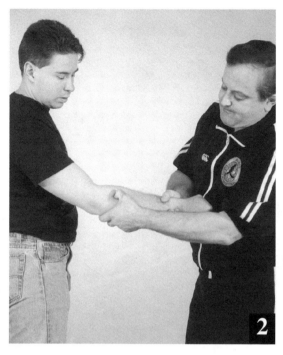
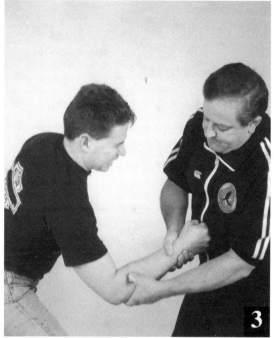

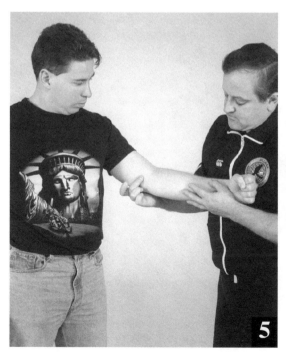
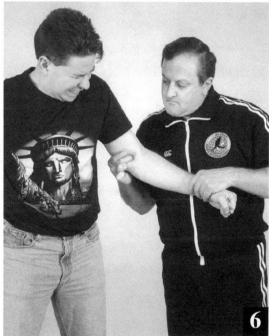

POINT NAME: Elbow Rub Point
(Triple Warmer # 11/TW-11)

LOCATION: TW-11 is found about 1
inch above the tip of the elbow on the
back of the arm [1].

METHOD: As its name implies, the
Elbow Rub Point must be rubbed up
and down, usually with the front of the
knuckles [2,3]. This point is a good one
to use in explaining how pressure points
work. When the Elbow Rub Point is
properly stimulated, a tiny tendon-nerve
cluster (called a Body of Golgi's) is
activated. This sends a false signal to
the spinal reflex, warning that the ten-
don at the elbow is about to tear away.
The body reflex causes the shoulder to
release and move away from the threat,
and relaxes the arm. As a result, the
elbow joint can be easily hyper-extend-
ed, and the attacker driven to the
ground [4-6].

VULNERABILITY: The Elbow Rub
Point is made vulnerable by touching
the Lower Wrist Point (H-6) and turning
the attacker's wrist outward, so the
thumb points down. It can also be
weakened by first attacking the Leg
Stomp Point (B-55, see page 94), or the
Lower Leg Point (Sp-6, see page 90).

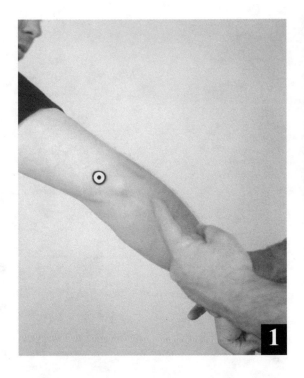

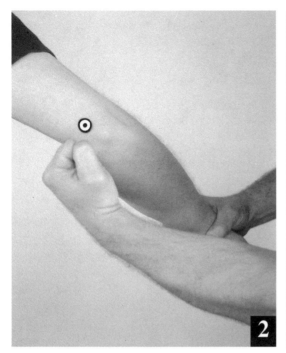

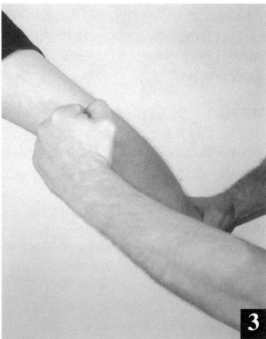

POINT NAME: Triceps Hit Point
(Triple Warmer # 12/TW-12)

LOCATION: TW-12 is located in the middle of the triceps on the back of the upper arm [1].

METHOD: Strike the Triceps Hit Point on a slightly rising angle to release the attacker's elbow and shoulder, and send him sprawling [2-5].

VULNERABILITY: The Triceps Hit Point is made vulnerable by touching the Lower Wrist Point (H-6) and twisting the attacker's wrist over. It can also be weakened by first attacking the Leg Stomp Point (B-55, see page 94), or the Lower Leg Point (Sp-6, see page 90).

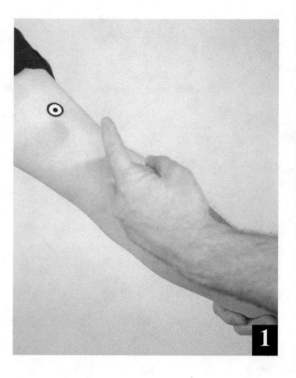

NOTE: When attacking the Triceps Hit Point from in front of an attacker (as shown in these photos) the wrist is turned so that the palm faces down. When attacking the point from the side (as shown on the next two pages), the wrist is turned so that palm faces up.

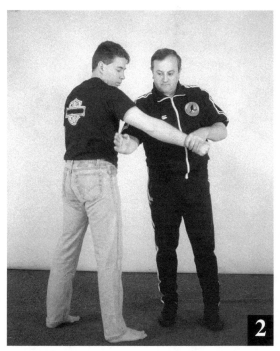

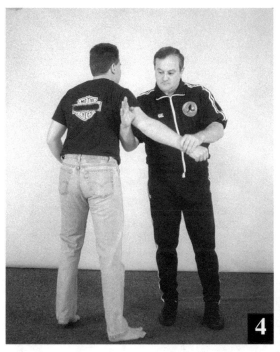

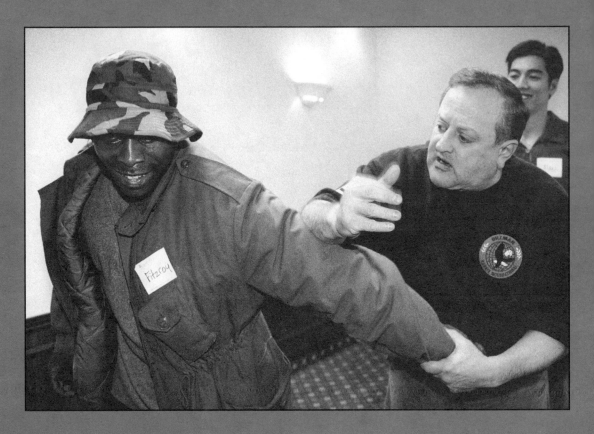

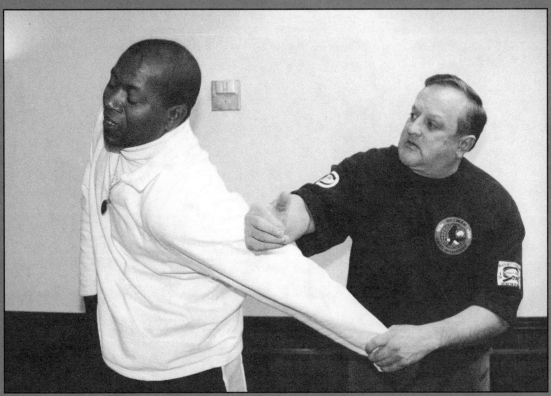

Pressure Point techniques are very effective on all types of people, even when they are wearing heavy winter clothing. But, pay special attention in these photos to the way in which George Dillman turns the subject's wrist when using the Triceps Hit Point (TW-12).

POINT NAME: Jaw Stun Point
(Stomach # 5/S-5)

LOCATION: Along the bottom of the jaw there is a slight indentation or notch at about the place the jaw muscle ends. This is the location for S-5 [1].

METHOD: Strike this point diagonally up and in. Use an open palm, and hit with a slight twisting motion [2,3]. Properly struck, a light blow to this point will stun the head (the sensation has been compared with receiving a boxer's powerful hook) and cause the legs to stagger. A more serious attack produces unconsciousness.

VULNERABILITY: The Jaw Stun Point is made vulnerable by attacking the Outer Forearm Point (LI-10), or the Inguinal Crease Points (Sp-12 & Li-12, see page 88). This point is also weakened by the consumption of alcohol.

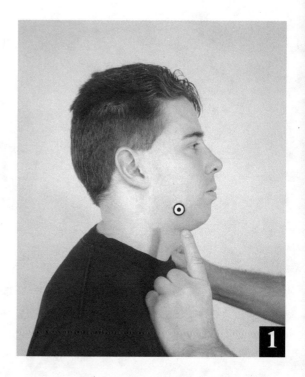

POINT NAME: Head Stun Point
(Triple Warmer # 17/TW-17)

LOCATION: TW-17 is found in the hollow of the jaw below the ear [4].

METHOD: Strike the Head Stun Point diagonally from back to front to cause dizziness, disruption of vision and unconsciousness [5,6].

VULNERABILITY: Weaken the Head Stun Point by attacking the Inner Arm Point (H-2) or the Lower Leg Point (Sp-6, see page 90; also, refer to page 112).

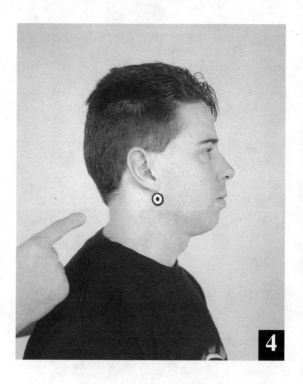

NOTE: When striking the Jaw Stun Point with the left hand [2,3], women should lift their left heel off the floor, while men should have their left foot firmly planted (vice versa on the right side). This is due to the *yin/yang* of women and men.

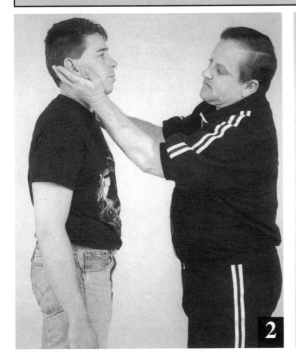
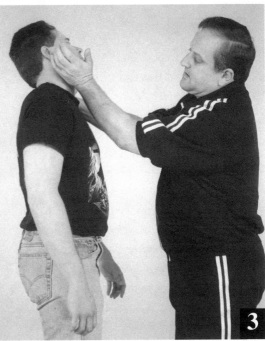

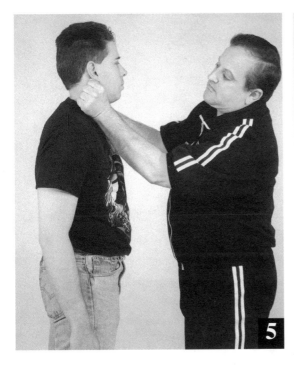
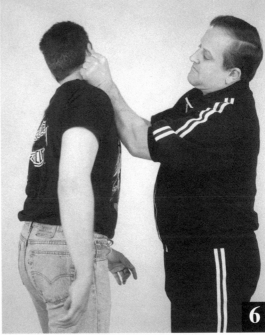

POINT NAME: Supra-Sternal (Jugular) Notch Point (Conception # 22/Co-22)

LOCATION: Co-22 is found in the hollow notch at the top of the sternum [1].

METHOD: With two fingers press in and down to drive an attacker away and produce a gag reflex [2-5].

NOTE: The Supra-Sternal Notch Point must be attacked in a downward direction. If you push in and up, you will miss the pressure point and attack the larynx which is a vital target.

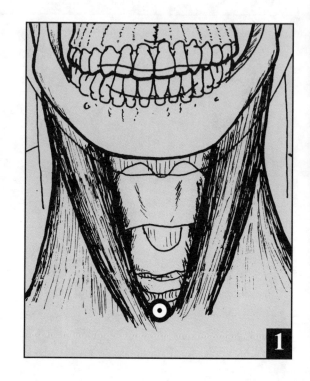

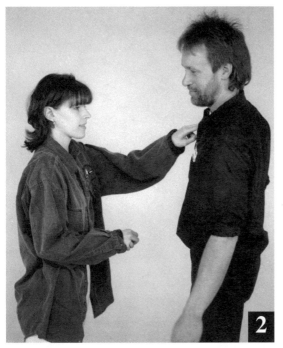
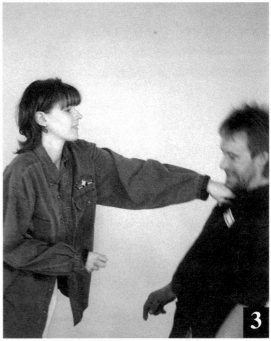

POINT NAME: Inguinal Crease Points
(Spleen # 12/Sp-12 & Liver # 12/Li-12)

LOCATION: The Inguinal Crease
Points are two side-by-side points found
in the crease of the thigh just lateral to
the groin [1].

METHOD: Strike these points downward and outward to bend an attacker
over and turn him to the side [2,3].

VULNERABILITY: The Inguinal
Crease Points can be weakened by first
attacking the eyes (a vital target) or
striking the Jaw Stun Points (S-5) on
both sides of the head simultaneously.

POINT NAME: Outer Thigh Point
(Gall Bladder # 31/GB-31)

LOCATION: GB-31 is found on the
side of the thigh, one third of the distance up from the knee [4].

METHOD: Strike from the outside
inward to buckle the leg and produce
painful cramping of the muscle [5,6].

VULNERABILITY: Weaken the Outer
Thigh Point by first attacking the Head
Stun Point (TW-17). This point is very
vulnerable in an individual who is on
the drug PCP.

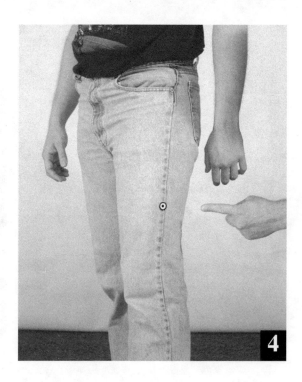

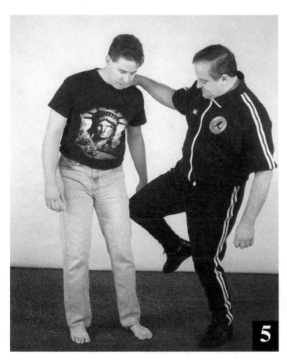

POINT NAME: Inner Thigh Point
(Spleen # 10/Sp-10)

LOCATION: Sp-10 is located on the inside of the thigh, about a hand-width above the knee [1].

NOTE: There are actually three points about a hand-width apart on the inner thigh — points which can be attacked interchangeably. A kick to this area is certain to hit at least one. Above Sp-10 is Sp-11, and behind it is Li-9 [1].

METHOD: Strike diagonally outward to collapse the leg [2,3].

VULNERABILITY: The Inner Thigh Point can be made vulnerable by an attack to the eyes (a vital target), the Upper Mid-Forearm Point (L-6), or the Jaw Stun Point (S-5). The inner thigh point is very weak in an individual who is on the drug PCP.

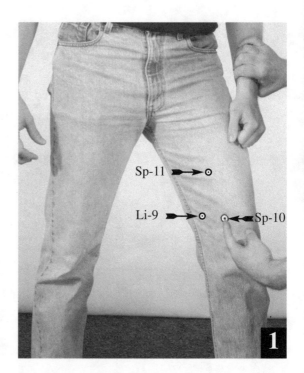

POINT NAME: Lower Leg Point
(Spleen # 6/Sp-6)

LOCATION: Sp-6 is on the inside of the leg, midway between the ankle bone and the bottom of the calf muscle [4].

METHOD: Strike from the inside outward to collapse the ankle and buckle the leg [5,6].

VULNERABILITY: To weaken the Lower Leg Point, attack the Inguinal Crease Points (Sp-12 & Li-12; refer to pages 222-225 for an example).

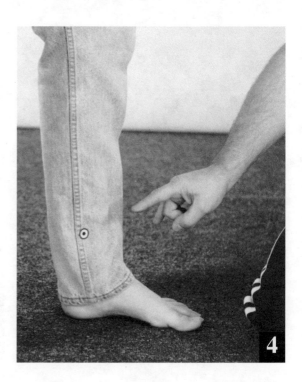

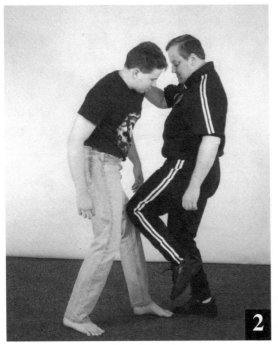

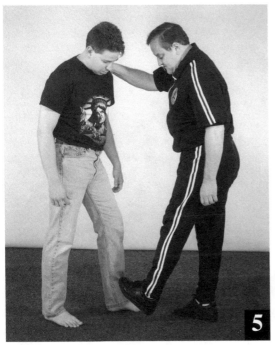

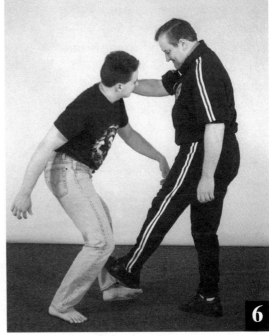

POINT NAME: Instep Point (Gall Bladder # 41/GB-41)

LOCATION: GB-41 is located between the foot bones leading to the fourth toe and the little toe, near the rounding of the instep [1].

METHOD: A stomp to the foot can be painful, but does not produce enough of an effect for self-defense purposes [2]. However, by striking the Instep Point diagonally inward, and attacker can easily be brought to his knees [3-5].

VULNERABILITY: Weaken the Instep Point by first attacking the Head Stun Point (TW-17). You may also attack the Instep Point as a way of weakening the Head Stun Point.

NOTE: The photos show how easy it is to put someone down using just a knuckle to attack the Instep Point. However, this is for demonstration only. In self-defense, the Instep Point is attacked with a stomp [6].

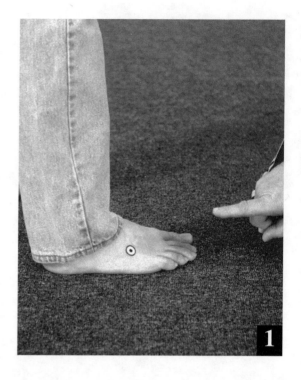

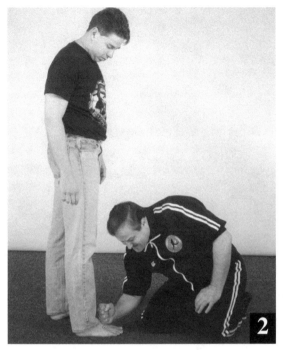

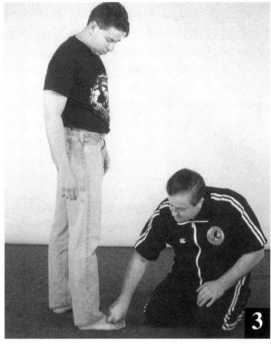

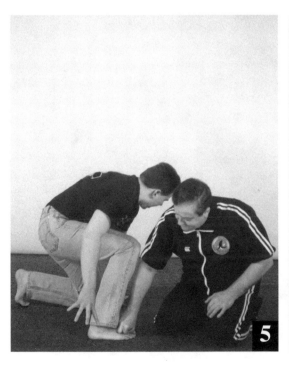

POINT NAME: Leg Stomp Point
(Bladder # 55/B-55)

LOCATION: B-55 is located on the
upper surface of the calf muscle, below
the crease of the knee [1].

METHOD: Stomp straight down on
this point to collapse an attacker's leg.
When one leg is collapsed, the other
will involuntarily kick out [2,3].

*NOTE: It is sometimes taught that one
should stomp into the crease of the
knee. But, while this will buckle the
knee, it causes the attacker's leg to fold
around the defender's foot.*

VULNERABILITY: The Leg Stomp
Point can be weakened by a strike to the
Jaw Stun Point (S-5).

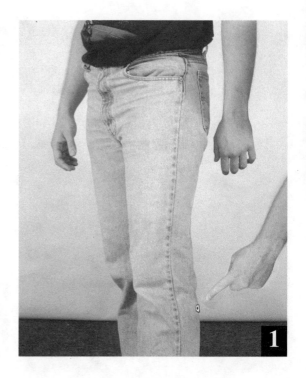

ADVICE ON ATTACKING PRESSURE POINTS

It does take practice to develop the right feel for pressure point self-defense. However, if you keep the following two pieces of advice in mind, you will have better success: 1) stretch it before attacking it; 2) attack with torque.

You will get a bigger response from a pressure point if you first stretch out your target. Many of the points for weakening which we have described work by causing the body to do just this. For example, if you strike the Outer Forearm Point (LI-10) the attacker's jaw will thrust forward, thereby stretching out the Jaw Stun Point (S-5). You could create a similar effect by grabbing the attacker's hair and pulling his head back.

To use torque means to somehow wiggle, grind, twist or otherwise manipulate a point as you attack it. When you step down on the Instep Point (GB-41), don't just step, grind. When you touch the Lower Wrist Point (H-6) give a little twist as you do it. When you kick the Inner Thigh Point (Sp-10) don't just kick, put a slight hook into your motion. In this way you will make it more difficult for the attacker to resist the effect of your pressure point technique.

"Pressure point self-defense has literally saved my life."

Darwin Banister
Elite Law Enforcement Training, Inc.
White Lake, MI

CHAPTER FOUR: Civilian Self-Defense

From a simple description of an attack it is impossible to determine the actual level of threat. In one circumstance, a punch to the face may not represent a significant danger to you, and "turning the other cheek" may be enough to diffuse a situation. In another circumstance, a punch might represent deadly force. Therefore, the type of response you use in self-defense is not measured by the particular attack leveled at you. Rather, you must decide how much force to use based on your perception of the threat. If you reasonably believe that you are in danger of suffering serious bodily harm, then you are morally justified if you injure your assailant in your self-defense.

However, you are never justified in "punishing" your attacker. Once an attacker is no longer a threat to you, you are morally (and legally) obligated to stop your counter-attack and make your escape. The legal principle of self-defense is that the level of response must be appropriate to the level of threat.

It should be noted, however, that over-kill is a necessary tactic in the context of military engagements. Regardless of the type of attack leveled, the response is always the same — "neutralize" the enemy. And the term "neutralize" is a euphemism for "kill or cripple." Even in a civilian context the same strategy may be appropriate, especially when threatened by multiple attackers.

Fighting against two attackers is not twice as hard as fighting against one; it is four times as hard! This degree of difficulty increases exponentially until you are faced with a group of around five (at which point the attackers start to get in each other's way.) This means that it is extremely difficult to successfully defend against multiple assailants. Furthermore, the psychology of a group attack practically guarantees that you will be seriously injured or killed if you do not escape. One of the few effective strategies in such a circumstance is to cripple or kill the closest member of the group (preferably the leader) with such sudden ferocity and viciousness that other attackers hesitate long enough for you to run away.

Obviously, in such a circumstance "humane self-defense" — defined as "effectively protecting yourself without causing serious bodily harm to your assailant" — is impossible. This means that solutions to multiple attacker scenarios are beyond the scope of this book. The reader may refer to our book **Advanced Pressure Point Grappling — TUITE´**, pages 270-277 and 342-349 for examples of humane techniques against two attackers. However, it should be noted that these techniques are "high skill" and require martial arts training.

In the following pages, we offer pressure point solutions to common self-defense situations. All of these responses are truly humane. They pose little threat of injury to the attacker. However, they are extremely effective because they are based on the sound principles and strategies which we have outlined already. It must be stressed that the humane responses presented are appropriate for the level of threat represented in each scenario. (This is not intended as a legal opinion, simply a reasonable conclusion.) It is only in chapter five — Law Enforcement Techniques — where we have shown humane solutions in circumstances where lethal force is justified.

As you study and practice, bear in mind that it is impossible to present all of the variables which a real street encounter can involve. A technique which we show here, which works beautifully in training, may fail on the street because of some unpredictable factor. These variables can be as diverse as the clothing you or your attacker are wearing, the weather conditions, how frightened or confident you feel, how frightened or confident your assailant feels, the condition of your or the opponent's health, and so on. For this reason, we recommend that you practice under as many different circumstances as possible, and with a variety of training partners. Also, train under the supervision of a qualified instructor.

It is important to practice mentally as well as physically. Vividly imagine self-defense scenarios. Try to conjure up the emotional intensity of such a situation. If you have experienced threatening situations in the past, relive them in your imagination, intentionally changing how you feel and how things turn out (picture yourself confident and victorious.)

The first three techniques we show represent three levels of response to the same physical assault. What makes the difference in the three responses is the level of perceived threat. They also illustrate the versatility our methods in real life.

Though self-defense is serious business, most people find the practice of Humane Pressure Point Self-Defense to be quite enjoyable – even when it hurts.

TECHNIQUE # 1

1. An assailant has grabbed your right wrist with his right hand. His grab is unwelcome, but you do not believe he represents a serious threat to your safety.

2. Bend your elbow and circle your right hand, drawing it in towards your strength. At the same time, shift or step slightly forward and to the left.

3-6. With your left palm, hit his right forearm, knocking it away, as you pull your right hand tight to your body.

NOTE: The emphasis in this technique is on driving his arm away, not on pulling your hand free. The two-way action of pulling your right hand into your strength as you knock his hand away makes it easy to gain release. However, the circling motion of your arm is essential because it maneuvers the attacker into a bio-mechanically weak position.

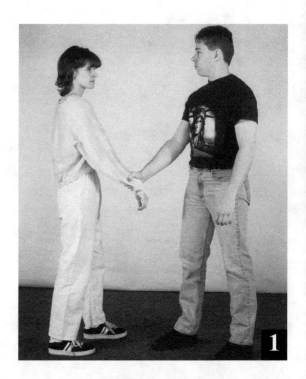

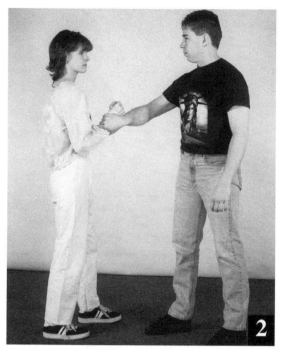

TECHNIQUE # 2

1. An assailant has grabbed your right wrist with his right hand. His behavior is pushy and aggressive. You feel that it is necessary to inflict pain to get him to release you and leave you alone.

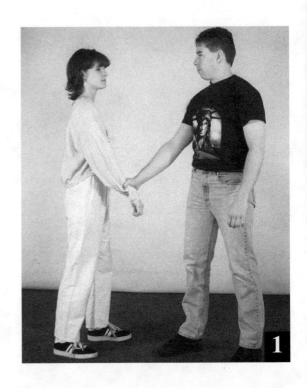

2. Shift or step slightly forward and to the left as you bend your right elbow, and roll your right fist into your strength. As your motion turns his arm, put pressure against his Lower Wrist Point (H-6) with the small knuckle of your fist.

3-5. Grind into his Lower Wrist Point (H-6) with your right fist as you strike down on his Outer Forearm Point (LI-10) with your left fist.

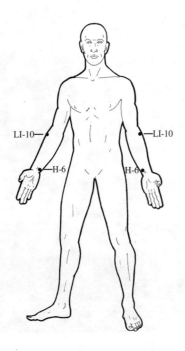

NOTE: Grinding your knuckle into the Lower Wrist Point (H-6) will weaken his grip on your arm. The strike to the Outer Forearm Point (LI-10) will cause a painful muscle spasm which can immobilize his arm for up to twenty minutes.

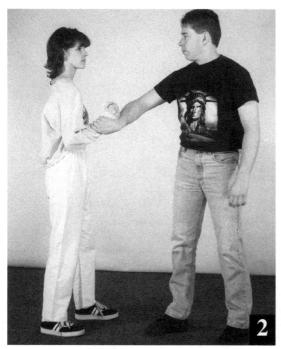

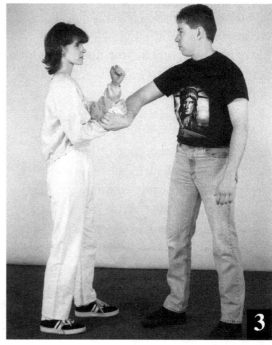

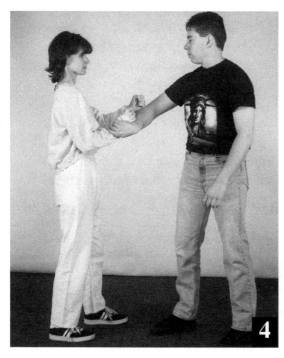

TECHNIQUE # 3

1. An assailant has grabbed your right wrist with his right hand. Because of his expression, threatening speech and demeanor, you believe he intends you bodily harm.

2. Shift or step slightly forward and to the left as you bend your right elbow, and roll your right fist into your strength. As your motion turns his arm, grind into his Lower Wrist Point (H-6) with the small knuckle of your fist.

3-5. In one motion, strike with your left fist at his Outer Forearm Point (LI-10), and stab at his eyes with the fingers of your right hand as it comes free from his grip.

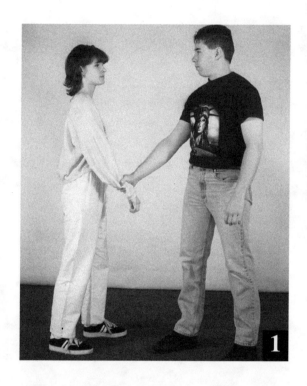

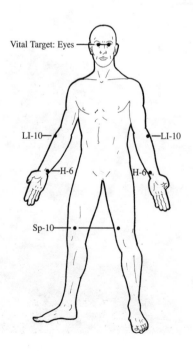

Vital Target: Eyes

LI-10 — — LI-10

H-6 — H-6

Sp-10 —

NOTE: It is important that you do not think of pulling your right hand out of his grip. Concentrate instead on attacking straight into his face. Because your attacker's eyes are well defended by blinking and flinching reflexes, it is unlikely that you will be able to cause him any damage. However, your intention must be to poke his eyes fiercely.

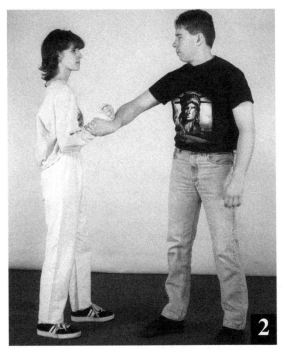
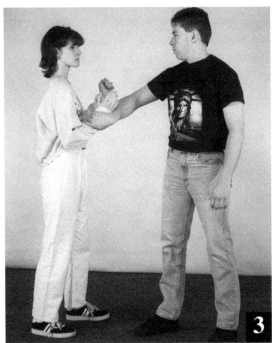

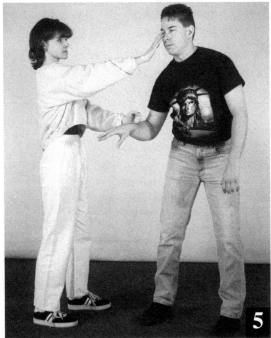

TECHNIQUE # 3 (Cont.)

6-9. With your right foot, kick his left leg forcefully, hitting the Inner Thigh Point (Sp-10). Run away without hesitation.

NOTE: As your attacker reacts to the strikes to his arm and eyes, he becomes momentarily unaware of the rest of his body. Your counter-attack serves as "...first attack east" for your follow-up kick to his leg.

When a woman is grabbed by a man she is usually outmatched physically. When a man is grabbed by another man it signals the beginning of a physical confrontation (i.e. a street-fight). In either case, the solution shown in technique # 3 is generally the most appropriate response. But, because circumstances do vary, the three levels of force which we have demonstrated take into consideration the ethical issues which surround self-defense.

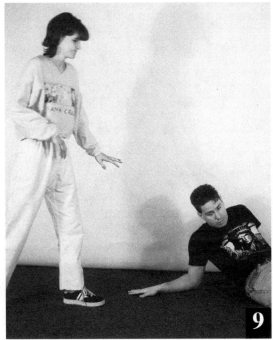

TECHNIQUE # 4

1. An assailant has grabbed your right wrist with his right hand.

2-3. Step forward and to the left as you bend your right elbow, and roll your right fist in towards your strength, and grind into his Lower Wrist Point (H-6) with the knuckle of your little finger to weaken his grip.

4-6. With your left hand near his elbow, and your right hand at his wrist, drive your attacker's arm across his own body, push him away and escape.

HINT: Try to drive your attacker's right elbow to the left side of his chest. This causes his arm to cross his centerline, which disrupts his balance.

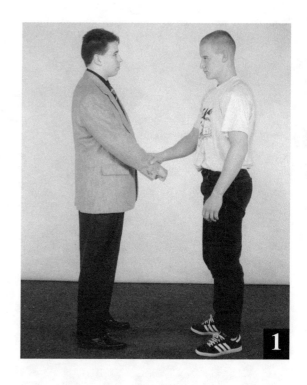

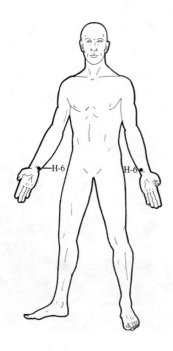

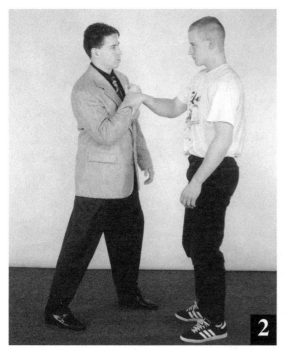

TECHNIQUE # 5

1. An assailant has grabbed your right wrist with his right hand, and is prepared to punch you in the face with his left hand.

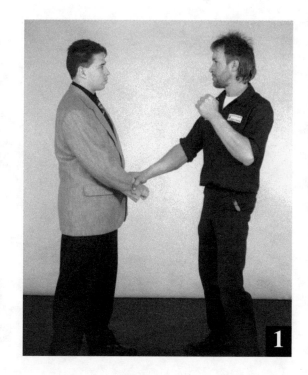

2-4. Without hesitation, pull your right hand towards your right hip as you kick the attacker at the Inner Thigh Point (Sp-11) of his left leg with your right foot.

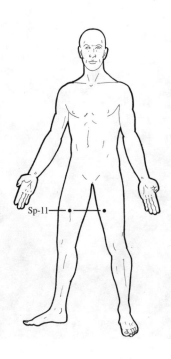

TECHNIQUE # 6

1. An assailant has grabbed your right wrist with his right hand, and is prepared to punch you in the face with his left hand.

2-3. With the tip of your left shoe, kick him on the Lower Leg Point (Sp-6).

4-5. Follow-up with a left palm strike to his right Head Stun Point (TW-17).

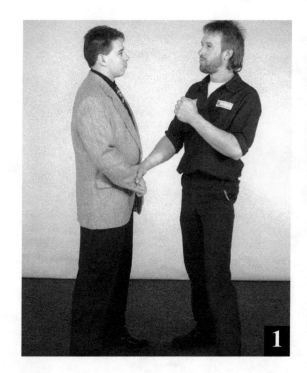

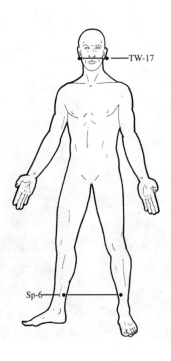

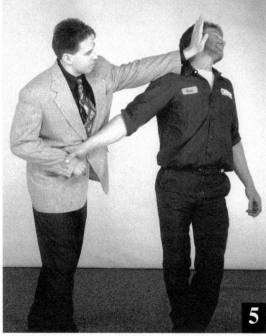

TECHNIQUE # 7

1. An attacker has grabbed on top of your left wrist with his right hand.

2-3. Do not pull away. Instead, step forward and to your left, bend your elbow, roll it over the top of his arm and press down.

4-5. Immediately lean your weight forward, driving your elbow into his chest.

HINT: As you roll your elbow, use his grab as your pivot point. Do not try to break his grip. Instead, focus on striking with your elbow.

6. Complete your defense with a right kick to the Inner Thigh Point (Sp-11) on his left leg.

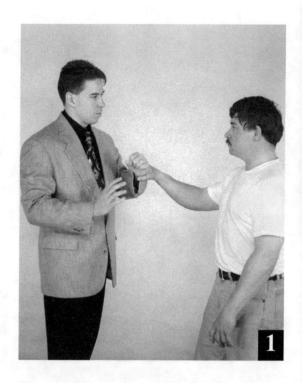

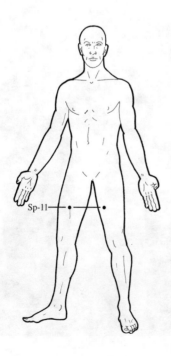

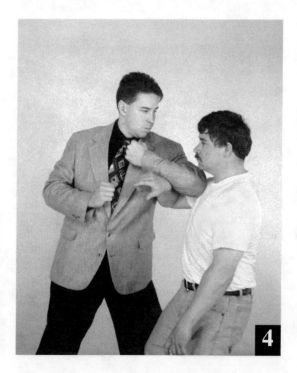

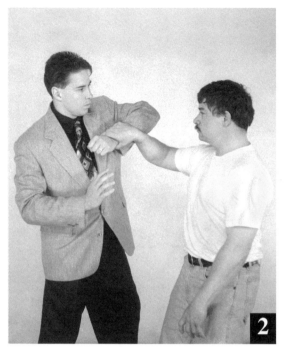

NOTE: This technique will work exactly the same way if your attacker has grabbed both of your arms, and even if he has grabbed one arm with both hands.

TECHNIQUE # 8

1. An attacker has grabbed the briefcase which you have in your right hand with his right hand.

2. Do not get into a tug-of-war for your briefcase. Instead, step forward and to your left, moving to the outside of his right arm.

3. Using your left forearm, strike against his Mid-Triceps Point (TW-12), to release his shoulder and bend him over.

4-6. With your left foot, stomp through his Upper Calf Point (B-55) straight to the ground to knock him down. Immediately make your escape.

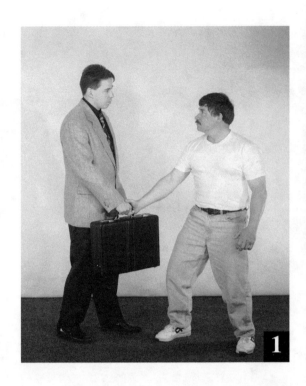

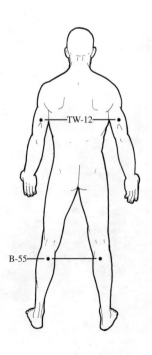

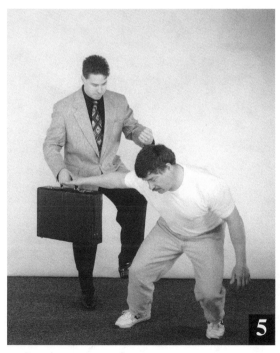
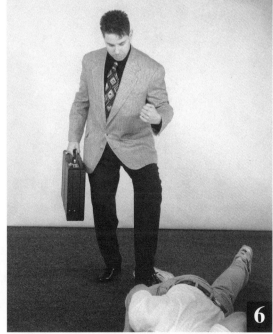

TECHNIQUE # 9

1. An attacker has grabbed the briefcase which you have in your left hand with his right hand.

2-4. Do not get into a tug-of-war for your briefcase. Instead, step forward with your right leg and strike the Outer Jaw Point (S-5) on the left side of his face with a twisting right palm.

NOTE: A woman should raise the heel of her right foot while striking the Outer Jaw Point as shown.

5-6. Move your left foot up one half step, and put your weight on it. Then strike with your right knee against the Inner Thigh Point (Sp-11) on your attacker's right leg.

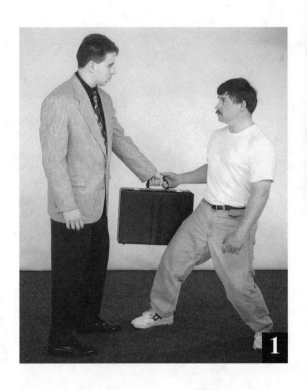

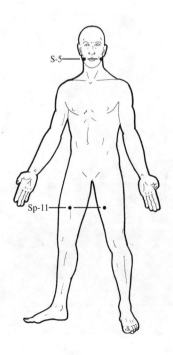

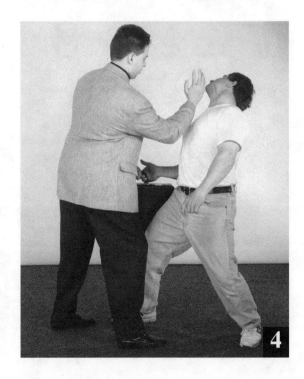

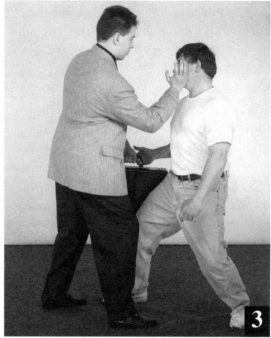

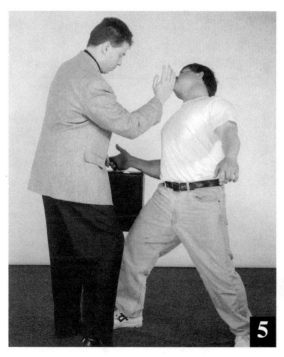

TECHNIQUE # 9 (Cont.)

7. Step towards your assailant after the knee strike, and grab him by the hair on the left rear quarter of his head.

8-10. Step back and to the right with your right foot. With a sharp motion, turn your attacker's head, and pull him to the ground. Then make your escape.

NOTE: Do not jerk the attacker's head, as this could injure his spine. Your move must be quick, decisive, but smooth.

NOTE: Whenever you make your escape from a self-defense situation, always keep alert for other assailants.

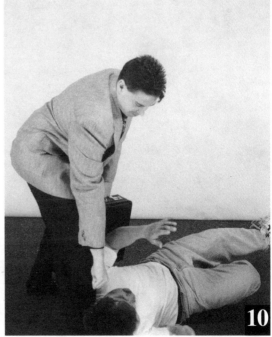

TECHNIQUE # 10

1. An assailant has grabbed you by both arms and is pulling you towards him.

2-3. Do not struggle or pull away. Instead, step forward and to your left, setting your left foot outside his right foot. When you do this, you are stepping outside of his power.

4-5. With your right knee, strike forcefully into the Inner Thigh Point (Sp-11) on his left leg.

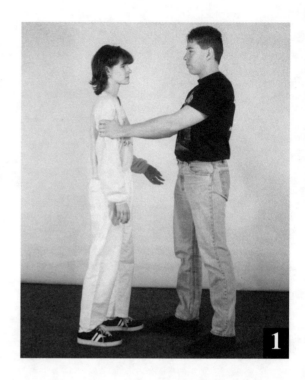

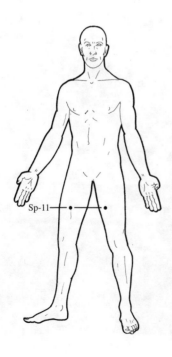

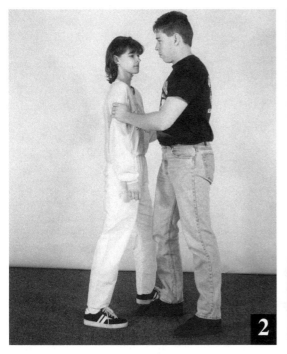

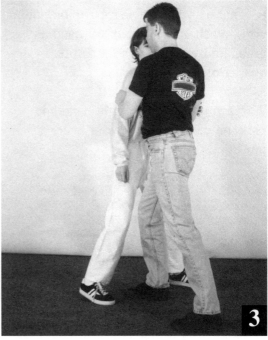

TECHNIQUE # 10 (Cont.)

6. Ignoring your attacker's grip on your arms, reach up with your left hand and grab him by the hair on the left rear quarter of his head.

7. Reach up with your right hand and press on the left side of your attacker's jaw.

NOTE: Be careful to keep your hand clear of his mouth.

8-9. Pushing with your right hand, and pulling with your left hand, take a step back with your left foot and spin the attacker around, dumping him on the ground.

10. Step away and make your escape.

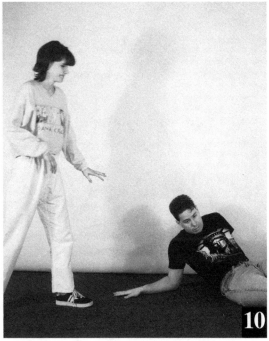

TECHNIQUE # 11

1. An obnoxious — but largely harmless — individual has grabbed your companion's right arm with his left hand.

2-3. Reach across with the fore-knuckles of your left hand and rub on the Upper Wrist Point (L-8) to release his grasp.

CAUTION: Be watchful for an attack coming from his right hand.

4-6. Quickly drive your palm against his upper sternum and knock him away.

> **NOTE**: It is best to leave at this point, to avoid any escalation of the confrontation.

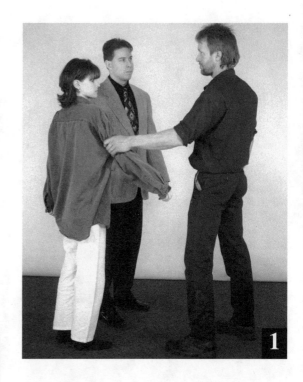

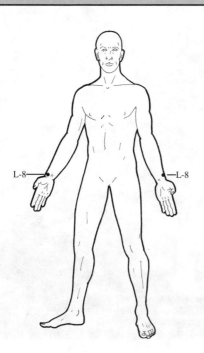

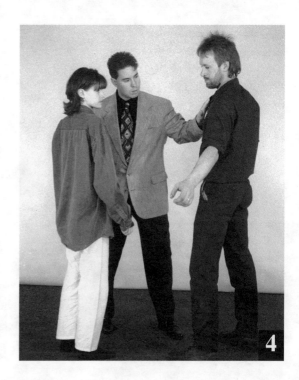

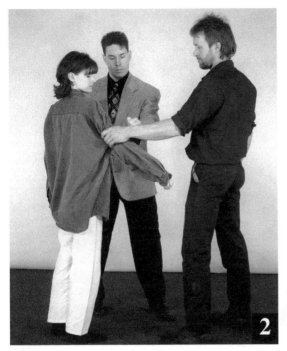

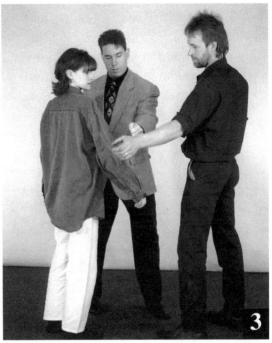

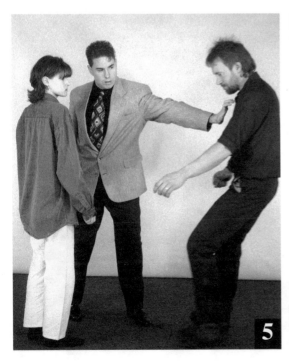

TECHNIQUE # 12

1. A highly agitated individual has laid his left hand on you and is waving his right index finger in your face. He is verbally threatening, and your attempts to diffuse the situation have failed.

2. With your left hand, catch his right wrist and squeeze the Upper and Lower Wrist Points (L-8 & H-6) with your fingers and thumb. Catch his index finger in the "V" between your right thumb and index finger.

3-4. With a hooking motion, bend his finger, sending him to the ground.

5. Drive his right elbow against the ground so that you have a strong base of support.

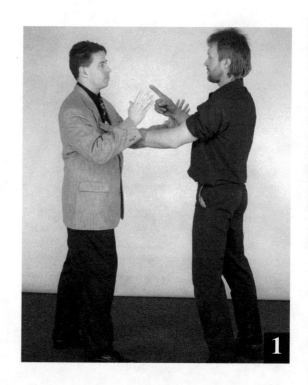

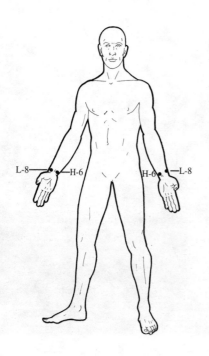

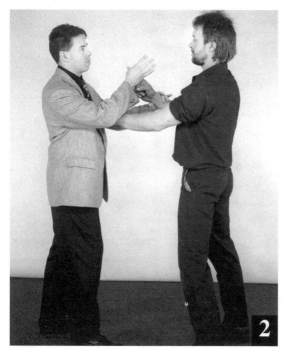

NOTE: At this point, you must make a strategic and ethical decision. If your response causes the assailant to experience a "change of heart," you may simply release him and leave. If he continues to threaten you, do not attempt to hold him in place and reason with him. Jerk his finger sharply towards his elbow (this will injure the finger), then run.

Finger control techniques are excellent for self-defense because they give you "range of force" options should the situation warrant a more serious response. And, even though a broken finger is "bodily harm," it still represents a fairly modest level of injury.

TECHNIQUE # 13

1. An attacker reaches for you with both hands.

2. Bring your arms up and press his arms inward so they cross. This momentarily disrupts his equilibrium.

3. With your right hand grasp the little finger of your attacker's right hand, bend it back and twist.

4-6. While bending and twisting his little finger, press down forcefully with one or two fingertips of your left hand on the Outer Forearm Point (LI-10), and send your attacker crashing to the ground. Then, escape before he can get up.

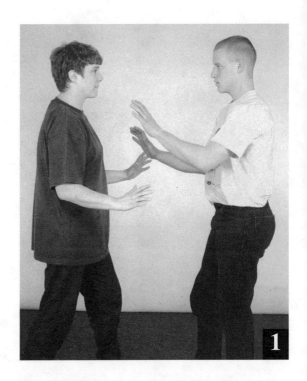

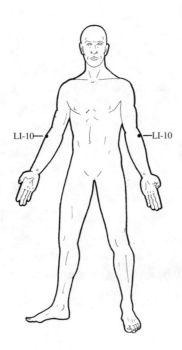

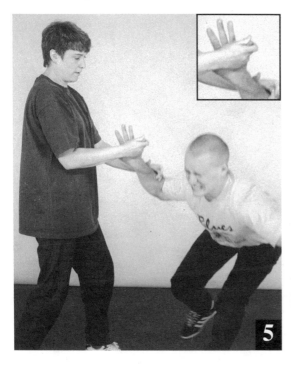

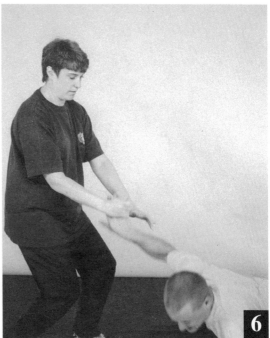

TECHNIQUE # 14

1. An assailant has placed his hands on you.

2-3. Bring your arms up outside of his, then strike inward with both arms, hitting your attacker's arms on the Outer Forearm Points (LI-10) and smashing his wrists together.

4-6. Strike upward against the Outer Jaw Points (S-5) with both hands to stun your attacker.

NOTE: Remember that strikes to the Outer Jaw Point are especially effective on assailants who have been drinking alcohol.

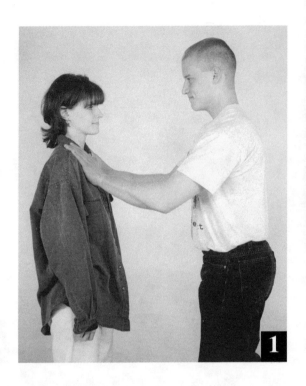

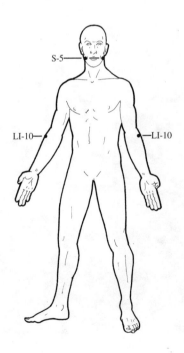

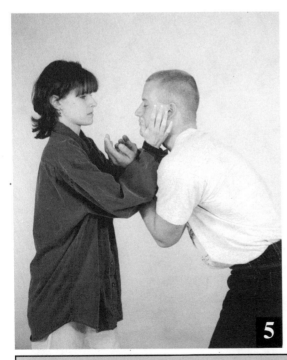
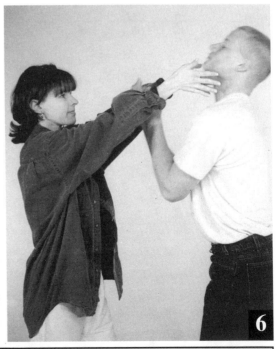

NOTE: When striking as shown, women should lift the heel of their lead foot off the floor, while men should have their lead foot firmly planted.

TECHNIQUE # 15

This is a unique technique for use against an attacker who is wearing a stiff-billed hat.

1. An attacker wearing a baseball cap has approached you unbidden and placed his hands on your hips.

2. Reach up and grasp the bill of his cap firmly, and press it straight into his forehead.

3-4. Grind the bill of his cap to the right and left across his forehead in a jerking motion.

5-6. Strike down onto his nose with the heel of your palm.

Note: When you rub his hat back and forth across his forehead, you are stimulating the supra-orbital nerve. The strike down on the nose stimulates the external nasal branch of the ophthalmic nerve (the anterior ethmoidal nerve). The result is a temporary inability to see properly, which gives you the opportunity to escape.

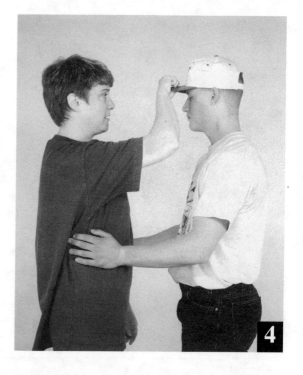

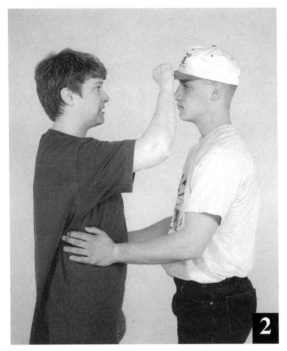

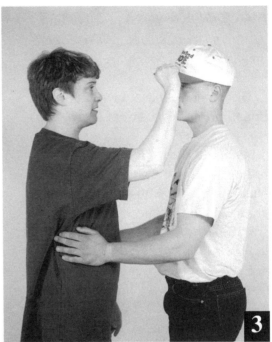

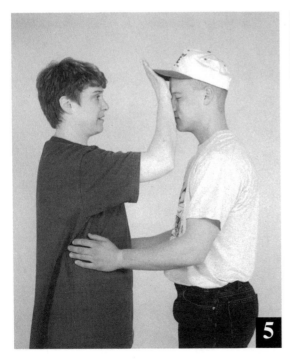

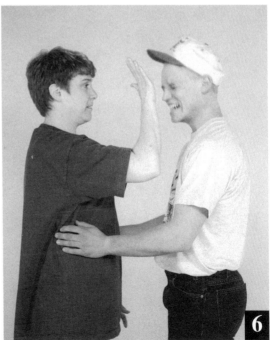

TECHNIQUE # 16

1. Someone has placed his right arm around your shoulders. His attention is unwanted and threatening.

2. Grind your left heel onto the Instep Point (GB-41) of his right foot.

3. As the attacker winces in pain, his head will drop down and his legs will buckle slightly. With your right hand grab him by the hair on the back left side of his head.

4. Pull down into your strength, turning his head and drawing him close. Grasp his chin with your left hand, keeping clear of his mouth.

5-6. Using both hands, spin your attacker's head, and pull him to the ground.

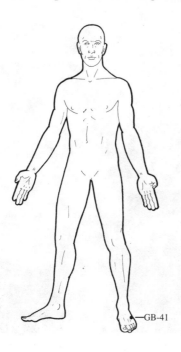

GB-41

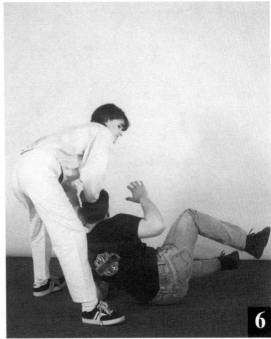

TECHNIQUE # 17

1. An aggressor has seized you by the lapels.

2. Because his hair is too short to grab, reach up with both hands and grab his ears.

3. Distract his mind from his ears by kicking him in the left Lower Leg Point (Sp-6) with the toe of your right shoe.

4-5. Step forward with your left foot and with a small, twisting action of your right hand on his left ear, turn your attacker's head to the left (his right).

CAUTION: Be careful to keep your forearm under his chin and away from his mouth.

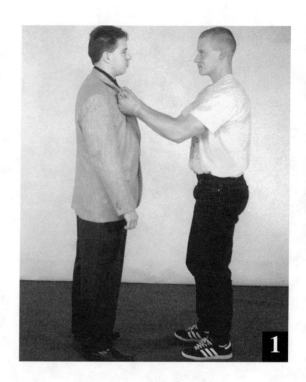

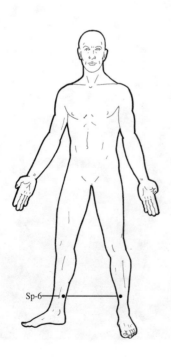

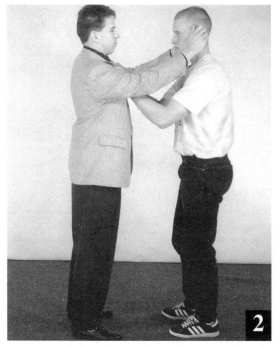

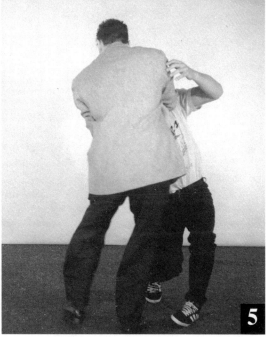

TECHNIQUE # 17 (Cont.)

6-7. As you continue spinning the attacker to your left, step back with your left leg.

8-9. Push the attacker's head down, causing him to fall away from you. This gives you the opportunity to escape.

HINT: As you turn your attacker's head, draw him close to your chest, into your strength, then project him away onto the ground.

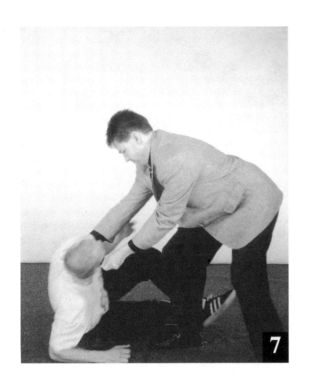

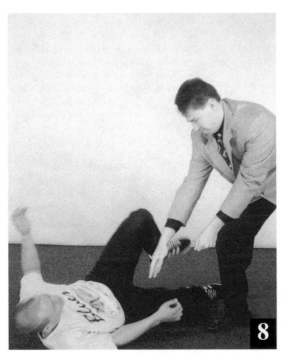

TECHNIQUE # 18

1. An assailant is beginning to choke you with both hands.

2. Do not try to knock his hands away. Instead, reach your left arm over both of his arms, and apply strong pressure with one or two fingertips to the Outer Forearm Point (LI-10) of his left arm.

3. Pull in towards your body — into your strength — trapping your attacker's hands against your chest.

4. Pinning his arms tightly to you, press into the Supra-Sternal (Jugular) notch Point (Co-22) with two fingers of your right hand.

5. Your attacker will start to push away from you to escape the pain.

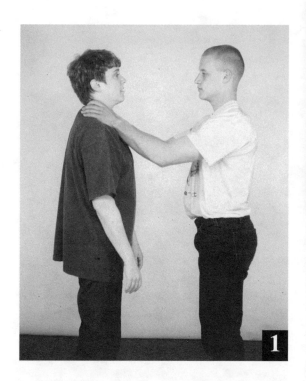

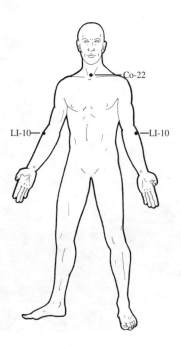

HINT: As you pull him in, draw his left elbow towards your center to disrupt his structure and weaken his hold on your neck. Once he starts to push away, you can follow-up with a right knee attack to the Outer Thigh Point (GB-31) on his left leg [5].

This technique depends on making your attacker do what you want him to do. He attacks, only to find himself trapped and in pain. Soon he will become desperate to escape.

Strategies like this one are important mentally in self-defense. They change your perception of a situation from helplessness to opportunity, from reactive to proactive, from victim to victor.

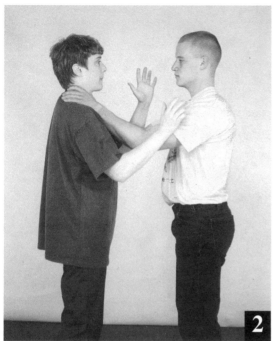

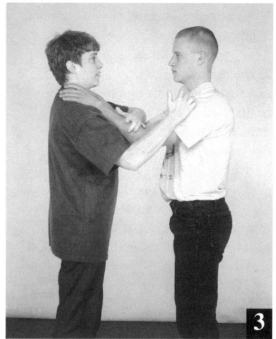

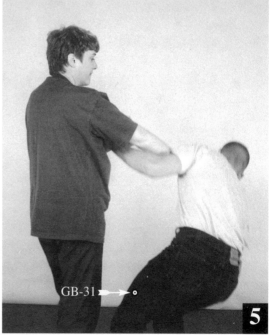

TECHNIQUE # 19

1. An assailant is choking you with both hands.

2. By grabbing your neck, he has exposed his little fingers to attack. Simply reach over with your left hand, grab the little finger of his left hand.

3. Bend his little finger back, and pull it across and behind his ring finger. At the same time, draw your forearm down towards your body, into your strength, as if to trap his arms against your chest.

4-5. Only when your assailant begins to fight to escape do you remove his hands from your body. Pull down on his little finger suddenly to project him to the floor. Then quickly escape.

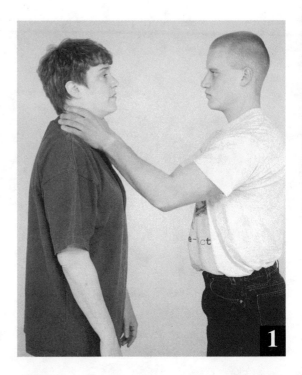

HINT: Once you have grasped his little finger, resist the temptation to peel his hand from your neck. If you do this, your attacker will simply pull away and attack you again. You must first trap him while inflicting severe pain. Then he will be trying to escape from you. So, do not think about escape, instead concentrate on your counter-attack.

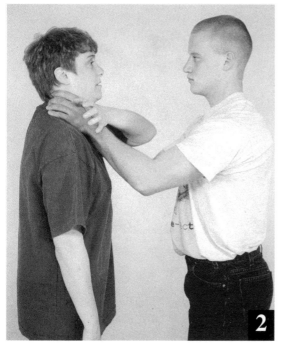

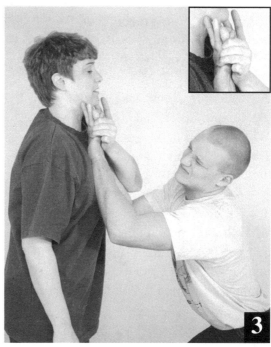

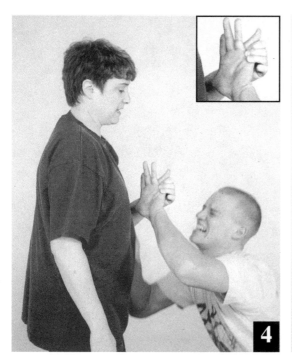

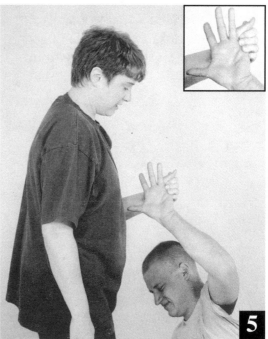

TECHNIQUE # 20

1. An attacker has grabbed you from behind in a bear hug, so that your arms are pinned to your body.

2. Bend your elbows and use your right hand to pin his left hand against you. With your left hand, grasp the little finger of his left hand and apply pain by bending and twisting it.

3. In response to the pain, your attacker will release you and attempt to pull away. Do not let him. Instead, continue to pin his left hand to your body, while bending and twisting his little finger.

4-6. Pivoting on your left foot, turn to your left with his hand still trapped against your body and his little finger bent. Your turning action will apply tremendous pressure against his finger, and send him forward, and away from you.

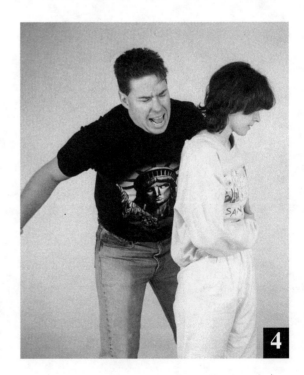

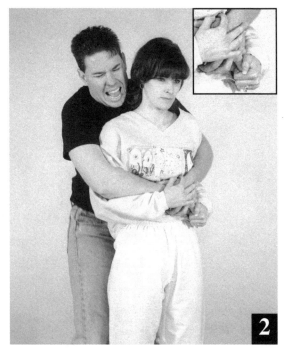

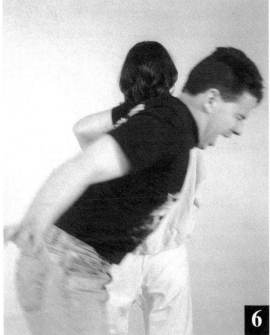

TECHNIQUE # 20 (Cont.)

A-E Details of this technique can be
seen from another angle.

A-B. As you pin the attacker's hand
while bending and twisting his little finger, you are waiting for him to react to
the pain. Do not hurry to turn or try to
escape. Concentrate on inflicting pain.
Make him want to escape from you.

C-E. As you make your turn to the left,
all you need to do is hold his hand
against your body. Your body pivoting
around his little finger gives you a
tremendous mechanical advantage. You
are using your strength against his
weakness.

*HINT: When you turn, use his bent lit-
tle finger as your pivot point. Be careful not to turn too quickly, or his finger
will simply break. It is the threat of
breaking that causes his body to move,
and it is the movement of his body in
one direction which gives you the
chance to escape in the other direction.*

*If you unintentionally break his fin-
ger, mercilessly wiggle and twist the
broken joint before running. This can
cause your attacker to faint, and at the
very least will leave him in anguish.
This may not sound like a very humane
thing to do, but, his finger will heal in 6
weeks, while your life can never be
replaced.*

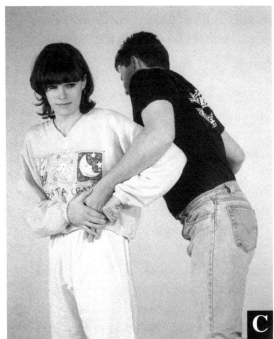

TECHNIQUE # 21

1. An assailant has approached you from behind and put a full nelson hold on you.

2. Reach back with your right hand and stab at his eyes with your fingertips.

NOTE: The stab at the eyes must be done with full intention to injure him. However, it is really only a distraction — a case of "...first go east" — for what you will do next.

3-5. Grab one finger of his right hand *(the little finger is best)* with your right hand and bend it back. Do not peel his hand off your neck. Instead, trap his hand against your neck, while bending and twisting his little finger. As his hold loosens, begin to pivot to the right.

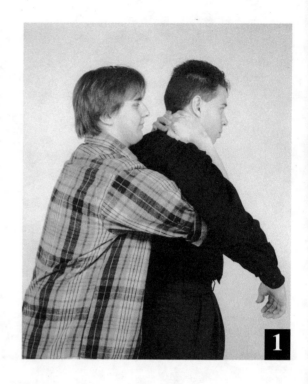

1

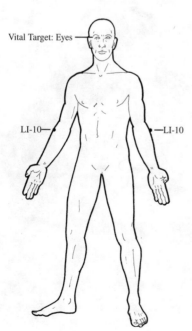

Vital Target: Eyes

LI-10 — — LI-10

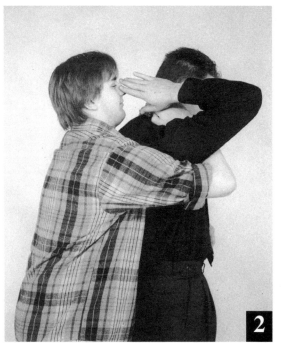

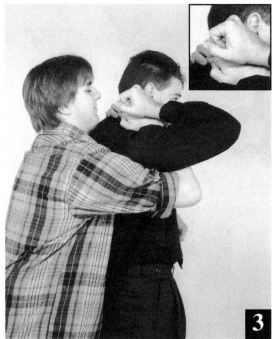

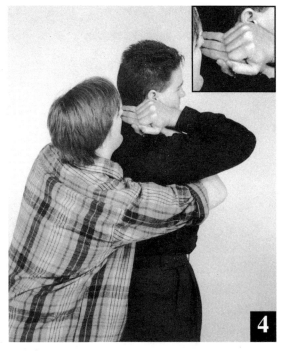

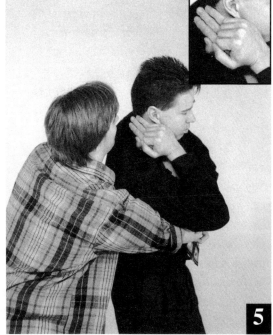

TECHNIQUE # 21 (Cont.)

6. In response to the pain, your attacker will release his hold, while you continue to use your right hand to trap his bent finger against your neck as you turn to face him. Grab his right arm near the elbow with your left hand, digging the tip of your thumb into the Outer Forearm Point (LI-10).

7-8. Maintaining your control on his little finger, slide the attacker's arm down your body. Do not pull him away, but continue to press him into you as you move him towards the ground.

9. Slide him down your leg until he is on the ground.

NOTE: As you slide his arm down, you are using your own body as a base against which his finger is trapped. At the start, you are basing him against your neck [5]. Then, you base him against your shoulder [6], your torso [7], your thigh [8], and so on, right to the ground. This is a smooth and continuous transition. However, if at any point the attacker begins to struggle, simply press him strongly against whatever part of your body you have reached, and wiggle his trapped finger. This will produce a sharp increase in his pain, and will "take the fight out of him." Then you will be able to continue the motion to the ground.

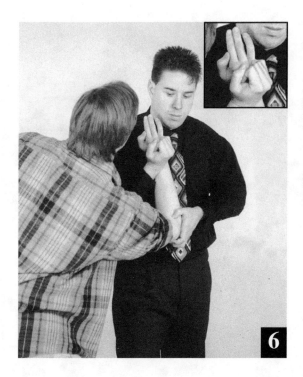

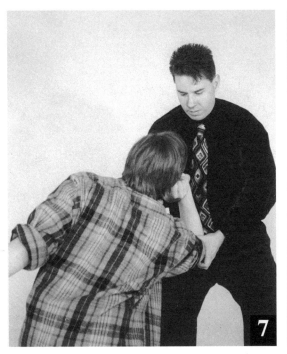

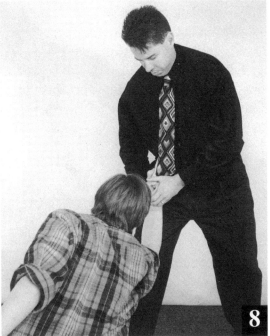

NOTE: Once the attacker is on the ground, you must make a difficult decision. If you believe that you are no longer in danger, let him go and escape. If you believe he is still a threat, use a sharp, downward motion to sprain his little finger, then run while he is incapacitated by pain.

Remember, it is never morally right to sprain his finger as punishment. You must reasonably believe that it is necessary to do so in order to protect yourself from bodily harm. You cannot read the assailant's mind, so you must use your own best judgment. However, when in doubt, it is safer for you to use the more serious technique.

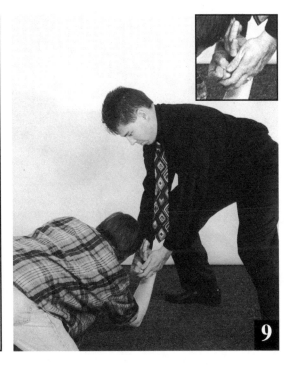

TECHNIQUE # 22

1. An assailant has grabbed your right wrist from behind with his right hand.

2. Take a half step back, toward(!) your opponent, bend your elbow, drawing into your strength, and trap his arm against your body with your arm.

3. Pull your right hand free, and grab his fingers with your left hand (forcing his little finger behind his ring finger).

4. Turn to your right while twisting his trapped fingers, and grasp his Wrist Points (L-8, H-6) with your right hand.

5-6. Twist and bend his fingers as you bring his forearm into your torso. This creates a base, making him helpless as you force him to the ground and escape.

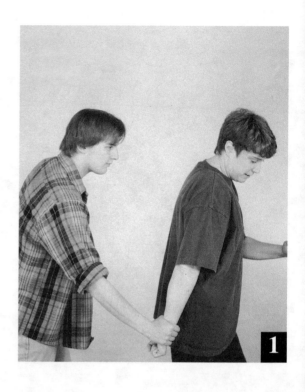

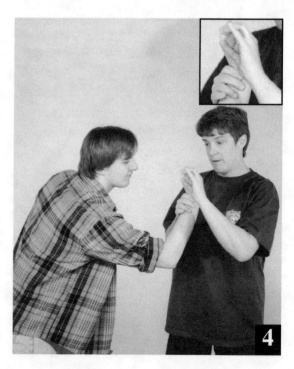

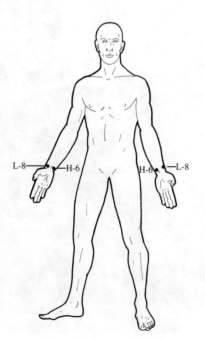

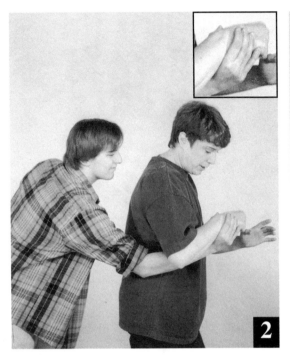

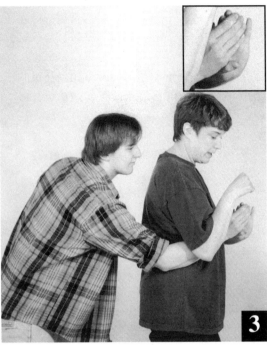

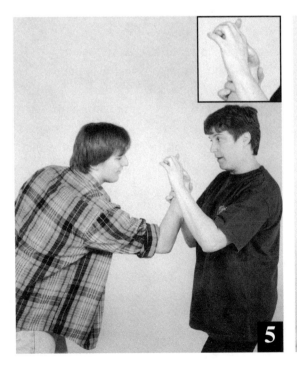

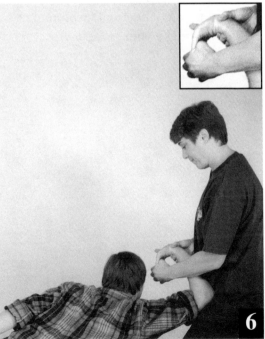

TECHNIQUE # 23

1. An attacker grabs you under your arms and lifts you off the ground.

2. Trap his right arm under your right arm by squeezing the muscles of your armpit.

3. With your right hand, pin his left hand to your body. *(Using only your right arm, you control both your attacker's arms.)* With your left hand, grab the little finger of his left hand, bending and twisting it.

4. In pain, the attacker will drop you and try to pull his hand away. Keep him pinned to you, applying pressure against his little finger.

5. Turn to your left, peeling his left hand from you only at the last moment before you make your escape.

NOTE: In many of the solutions we have given to situations involving grabs, the strategy you use is one of pinning the attacker to you, instead of pushing him away. When someone grabs you, your mental attitude should be, "You've got me right where I want you." Treat their aggressive action as an opportunity for your counter-technique, and make <u>him</u> want desperately to get away from <u>you</u>.

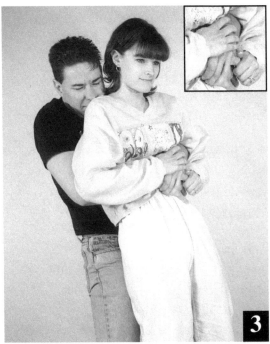

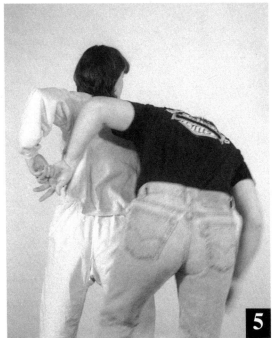

TECHNIQUE # 24

1. An aggressor has grabbed you from behind by your right shoulder.

2. Turn to your right, into the grab, and bring your right arm up to protect your head.

2-3. Smash down with your right elbow on the attacker's arm, hitting his biceps muscle *(as shown)* or the Outer Forearm Point (LI-10).

4-5. Strike with your fist under the attacker's right ear to the Head Stun Point (TW-17)

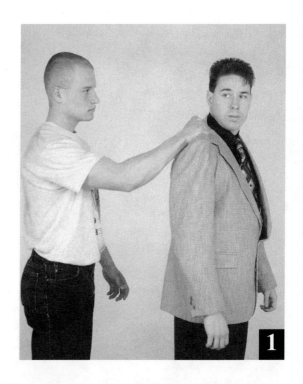

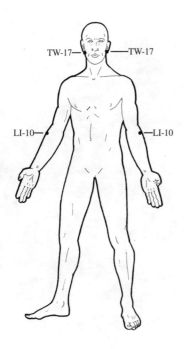

You will notice that we have not dealt with self-defense against a weapon wielding attacker. This is because an unarmed person will win only against a novice in a weapon verses empty-hand situation. And, as little as thirty minutes training can give an armed aggressor a huge advantage. As a result, when faced with a weapon, the best defense is to run.

Take special consideration of this principle when facing a gun. If an attacker threatens you with a gun, your best defense is to run. If an attacker with a gun threatens you, saying, "Come with me or I will kill you," **run!! NEVER, UNDER ANY CIRCUMSTANCES, SHOULD YOU ACCOMPANY THE ASSAILANT ANYWHERE! NEVER GET INTO THE ATTACKER'S CAR! JUST RUN!**

If someone with a gun jumps into your car with you and says, "Drive, or I'll shoot you," jump out of the car and run away. (A good strategy is to jump out of your car as you approach a red light. As you are braking, put the car in neutral, then jump out when the car is still moving, so that it will roll into the intersection while you escape.)

So, why do we recommend running instead of going with a gun-wielding attacker who might very well shoot at you if you run? Ask yourself this, which is the easier target, a frightened, screaming, running-for-your-life potential victim, or a tied-to-a-tree-after-being-raped-and-tortured actual victim? If you accompany a gun wielding attacker you almost certainly will be murdered. If you run like a mad fool, you *might* be fired upon, *possibly* even struck by a bullet, and *perhaps* even killed. Given the choice, it is better to risk possible death than to embrace certain death.

And remember, the only reason an assailant would use a weapon to coerce you to accompany him is because he does not feel safe to carry out his plan against you in the place the abduction attempt occurs. He needs to feel in control of his environment, so he seeks to take you to a place where he feels safe. If he doesn't feel safe to carry out his plans for your harm until he gets you to his lair, he may not feel safe enough to even fire his weapon at you if you run.

Small Circle Jujitsu, developed by Wally Jay, is a powerful, effective, and humane form of self-defense. A close, dear friendship exists between Professor Jay and author George Dillman. Professor Jay incorporates the Dillman Pressure Point Method in his jujitsu, while George Dillman has made Small Circle theory a central concept of his pressure point practice. Among those securing the future of Small Circle Jujitsu is Professor Jay's son, Leon, featured in this photo.

"Dillman's system is the missing link in unarmed defensive tactics for police and special operations."

Ray Mirabile
Defensive Tactics Instructor
Chicago, IL

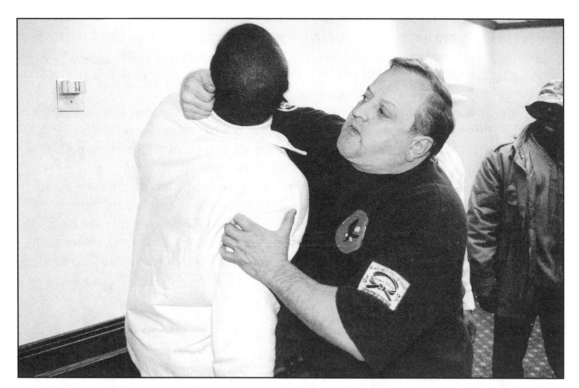

CHAPTER FIVE: Law Enforcement Techniques

If the goal in civilian self-defense is to escape from an assailant, the goal of Law Enforcement Defensive Tactics is to control and arrest the subject. In this setting, the need for humane yet effective methods is greatly increased.

In recent years, the number of lawsuits brought against police officers and departments for use of excessive force has increased. This is partly do to changes in society, changes which hold police to a higher standard of behavior than the criminals they are called to apprehend. It is also partly due to economic cutbacks which have reduced the number of officers on duty. Where police at one time traveled in pairs, increasingly squad cars have a single officer. And though the squads are intended to back each other up, they can actually be miles apart when an incident arises. (This is especially true of Sheriff's departments in largely rural counties.) The result is that officers will sometimes use a higher level of force because they do not feel safe facing a subject alone.

Some departments have responded to the increase in lawsuits by increasing police officer training. Their feeling is that a better trained officer will make better decisions under stress. They also feel that if the officers have had proper training, the department can protect itself if an officer is accused of excessive force. The argument is that the department did everything reasonable to insure that the officer knew the rules of proper conduct and was properly trained to respond. If the officer did act excessively, he or she was clearly violating departmental training and policy.

Other departments, however, have taken a different approach. They have actually reduced training in defensive tactics. These departments reason that a police officer accused of excessive force, who was using the techniques taught in the approved train-ing course, creates increased legal exposure. The belief is that it is better to have a poor-ly trained officer injured and pay out Worker's Compensation, than to have a suspect injured and pay out in liability damages.

Either way, the modern police officer is in a difficult situation. Caught between the danger, threat and adrenaline of confronting dangerous criminals on the one hand, and the spectre of civil litigation and departmental abandonment on the other, police officers are increasingly finding that their jobs are a no-win situation.

It is our hope that, in some small way, the methods of *Humane Pressure Point Self-Defense* will be of benefit to the officer in harm's way. The following techniques are based on the best principles of pressure point fighting. These concepts and tactics have been proven on the street by police officers around the country. Law enforcement personnel, from street patrol to undercover officers, are effectively and safely controlling and arresting subjects with these methods.

DISTANCING AND POSITION

Civilian self-defense is based on the premise that an aggressor has penetrated one's safety zone ("personal space") and is either threatening harm or actually beginning to inflict it. In this setting, it is the attacker who effectively establishes the distance or "interval" between the attacker and the target. The wise civilian, sensing the possibility of danger, will always seek an advantageous distance and posture in the face of a threat. However, this is not always possible since the initiation of an encounter begins with the attacker.

In law enforcement circumstances, it is the officer who usually initiates contact with a subject. This means that the officer must enter into every encounter mindful of its poten-tially violent outcome, and take steps to insure his or her own success. One of the keys to this process is to secure an advantageous position in a manner which does not alert the sub-ject to what is being done.

The first element in this process is controlling the interval. Though most people do not appreciate this fact, distances involved in actual physical encounters are much different than what one would predict. A general rule of thumb is this: if you think you are a safe distance away from a potential threat, you almost certainly need to be further back, and if you think you are close enough to make a successful first move, you need to be closer.

For example, a person standing 20 feet away from a knife-wielding attacker would likely feel they were at a safe distance. However, police officers know that even at 20 feet there is still not have enough time to draw a side arm, take aim and fire before that attacker can close the gap and bring the knife to bear. 20 feet! At 15 feet an officer has virtually no hope of drawing and firing.

To be able to respond to sudden physical aggression, it is considered necessary to establish a distance of at least 9 feet (called the "Reactionary Gap") between the officer and the subject. On the other hand, if the officer is anticipating having to take action to arrest a subject, it is necessary to stand very close, almost in touch range (a range of 4 feet or less, called the "Critical Action Interval"). Stand too far away, and the subject will have time to react and a struggle will ensue. But, to stand within the CAI also puts an officer within the danger zone for the subject's sudden attack. So, during encounters which occur within this range, it is necessary to increase the officer's safety and preparedness by using positioning and posture.

Positioning refers to where an officer stands in relation to the subject. If we consider straight ahead for the subject to be represented by 12:00, then the officer should seek a position which is off that line, on the subject's 1:00 or 11:00. We have already mentioned that by taking a position to the outside of an opponent's arms, you are moving away from his strength. The 1:00 and 11:00 positions are chosen for exactly this reason.

Posture refers to the manner in which an officer stands. This stance must provide protection against a sudden attack, be ready for rapid engagement, protect the side-arm from seizure, and offer no apparent threat that might aggravate a tense situation. For this we recommend the Non-confrontational Ready Position. The hands are held up and open in an apparently casual and conversational manner, with the gun side to the rear. Weight is kept slightly on the back leg so that forward motion is facilitated.

The Non-confrontational Ready Position also has a psychological component. As the officer approaches the actual moment of physical action, his or her dialog with the subject should become calming and conciliatory. A subject will sense on an intuitive level that the officer is preparing to move. It is impossible to completely conceal the clues. However, the calming talk and apparently non-threatening posture sends a different message. This creates a conflict between the conscious mind that is reacting to the words, and the intuition which is sensing the danger. In the presence of this type of psychological dissonance, reaction time is slowed as decision making processes become paralyzed. In this way, the subject is thrown into a state of confusion precisely at the moment the officer moves, making the arrest much easier. This is an important point, but a difficult one for many police officers to appreciate. Police are trained to use the "Command Voice" — a strong authoritarian

Positioning & Posture

Standing within the Critical Action Interval, you can almost reach out and touch the subject. This means that when you move, he will not have time to respond. It also means that if he moves first, you will have a hard time reacting. Especially at this dangerous range, position yourself on a slight angle (1:00, as shown, or 11:00) to the opponent, away from his strength. Your weapon side should be to the rear, your weight on the back foot. Your hands are in a non-provocative but protective position, your voice and demeanor are calm and conciliatory. This is the attitude taken immediately before moving forward to undertake an arrest.

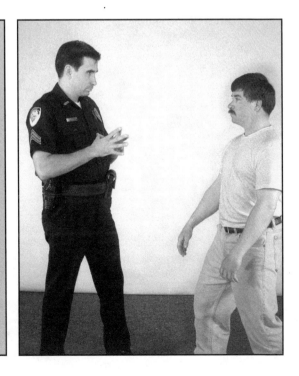

tone — to gain compliance. But, at the moment that a situation must escalate to a physical confrontation, the officer must stop using the command tones, and switch to calming talk. The command voice resumes, however, once the physical engagement has occurred. The sudden change from authoritarian to conciliatory to commanding speech generates further psychological confusion.

Calming talk also works to the benefit of the officer if the subject suddenly becomes aggressive. Because the subject has difficulty interpreting the state of readiness which the officer is in, he is unprepared for how quickly the officer will respond to his actions. Finally, and perhaps most importantly, the use of calming language and a non-confrontational posture can help to defuse a situation and keep it from escalating into a physical confrontation. An officer will never be injured if there is no physical altercation.

It should be noted that this psychological technique is essentially the same one used by some predators and bullies which we described in the context of civilian self-protection. The bully will sometimes use a friendly, joking, even polite and charming manner to confuse a potential victim's intuition, while he closes the distance and moves into the Critical Action Interval (the potential victim's personal space).

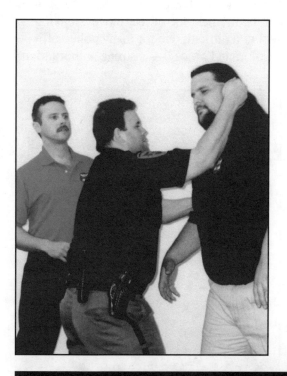 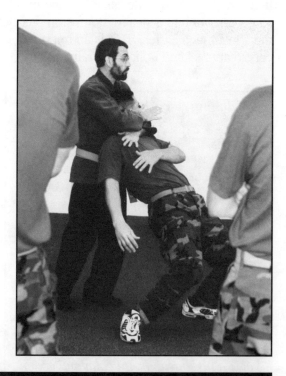

LEFT: Darwin Banister trains members of the law enforcement community in Humane Pressure Point Self-Defense
RIGHT: Author Chris Thomas works with a group of active duty U.S. marines.

Former Ultimate Fighting Champ (UFC), and Greco-Roman wrestling champ turned professional wrestler, Dan "The Beast" Severn, is a powerful and fearsome fighter. His size and physical presence are, to put it mildly, intimidating. However, even a warrior as powerful as Severn can be easily staggered by a light, but well-placed blow to a pressure point.

TECHNIQUE # 1
Come-Along

1. You are confronting an agitated, but non-violent subject, and standing within the Critical Action Interval (close enough to engage in one step).

2. Once it has become evident that the subject must be removed, you slide suddenly forward, leading with your left foot, to the outside of his right arm.

3. With your right hand, grasp his wrist from the outside, touching both the Upper and Lower Wrist Points (L-8 & H-6).

4-5. Grasp behind his elbow with your left hand and dig your fingertips into the Inner Arm Point (H-2) causing a pain reaction which lifts the subject up onto his toes.

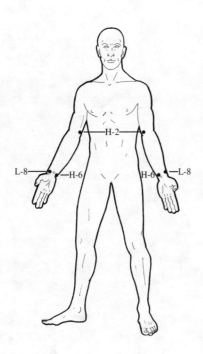

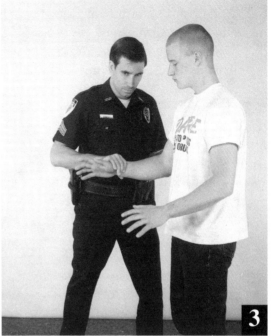

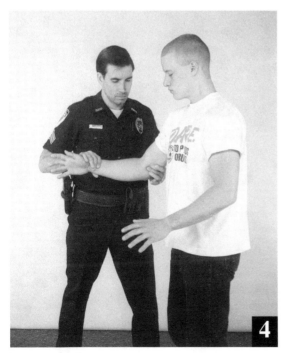

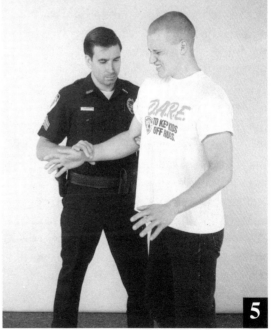

TECHNIQUE # 1 (Cont.)

6-7. Slide your left arm along the inside of his forearm. Bend his wrist downward (palmar flexion) and cradle his elbow in the crook of your left arm.

NOTE: As you slide your left arm up and bend his wrist, bump the back of his elbow from behind with the crook of your left arm. This creates a sharp shock in the wrist as the come-along is being applied and overcomes any resistance he may offer.

8. Apply torque and pressure to his bent wrist, using the pain to escort the subject in the desired direction.

Detailed Instruction

A-B. As you apply pressure to the Inner Arm Point (H-2) wiggle your fingertips to cause maximum stimulation and reaction. At the same time, twist the fingers of your right hand against the Wrist Points (L-8 & H-6).

C. After you have bent his wrist, turn his fingers to the outside of his body (in this case, you turn his fingers to point to his right.) Do not apply a steady and continuous pressure to his wrist. Rather, use an irregular, pulsating pressure while talking in a very calm voice. If you see any signs of panic in the subject reduce the level of stimulation you are applying to his joint. (If he panics he will begin to fight wildly, and you will find yourself in an escalating force situation.)

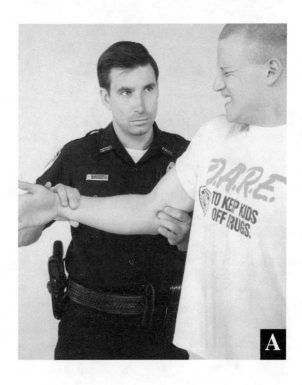

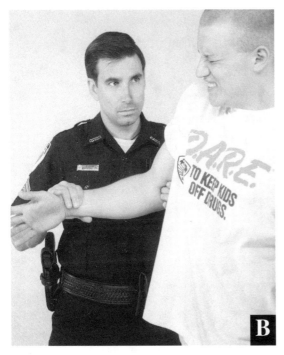
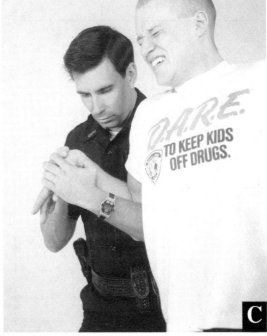

TECHNIQUE # 2
"Active-Resister" Take-Down and Cuff

1. You are standing within the Critical Action Interval of an aggressive subject.

2. Slide suddenly forward to the outside of his right arm.

3. With your right hand, grasp and pull his wrist, touching both the Upper and Lower Wrist Points (L-8 & H-6). With your left hand, seize behind his elbow, digging your fingertips into the Inner Arm Point (H-2).

4. Push down on his wrist with your right hand, and use painful pressure on his Inner Arm Point (H-2) to raise his elbow up .

5-6. Rub the Elbow Rub Point (TW-11) with your left wrist. Then press down against his elbow with your left forearm while pulling his wrist towards your right hip with your right hand.

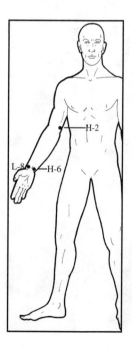

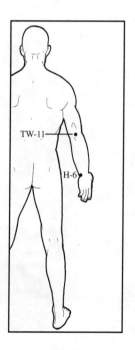

TECHNIQUE # 2 (Cont.)

7-8. As you drive him towards the ground, step back with your right foot and pivot on your left foot to your right so that the subject falls in a slightly circular path, with your body as the axis.

NOTE: As you are performing steps 5-8, use a loud and commanding voice, saying, "FACE DOWN ON THE GROUND, RIGHT NOW!" Your voice is one more source of stimulation which breaks down his resistance.

9. With the suspect on the ground, use both hands to bend his right wrist back, while saying, "PUT YOUR HANDS BEHIND YOUR BACK! DON'T RESIST AND YOU WON'T BE HURT!"

10-12. Kneeling on his right shoulder with your right knee, and his right hip with your left knee, proceed with handcuffing.

NOTE: Do not kneel on his spine.

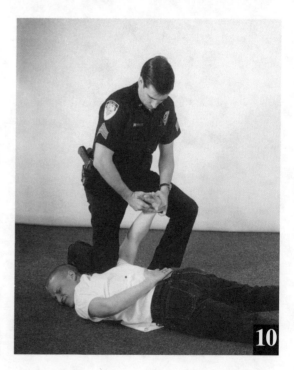

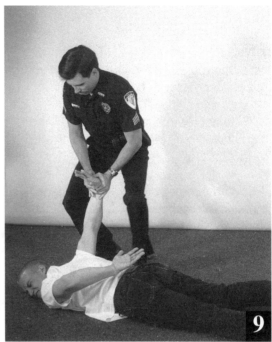

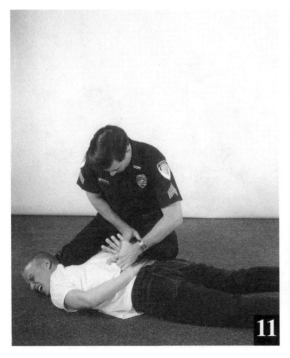

TECHNIQUE # 3
Disengaging From an Aggressive Subject

1. You are conducting a field interview, when the subject becomes aggressive and reaches for you with both hands.

2-3. Do not try to knock his hands outward, but instead knock his hands inward so that his arms cross.

4-6. With the subject's arms crossed, he is momentarily unbalanced. Take advantage of this by slipping your right hand over his crossed arms so that your forearm traps his arms as you push him strongly on his upper sternum. As he is propelled back, you have created space in which to act. You may draw your weapon, retreat and wait for back-up, or try to talk the subject down, as the situation warrants.

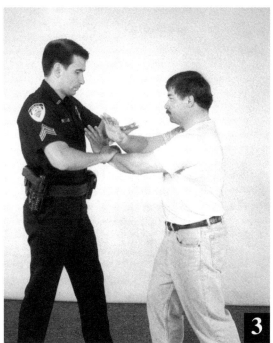

TECHNIQUE # 4:
Arresting an Aggressive Subject

1. You are conducting a field interview when the subject becomes aggressive and reaches for you with both hands.

2-3. Knock his hands inward, crossing his arms right over left.

4. Slip your right hand over his crossed arms so that your forearm traps his arms as you push him on his upper sternum and stop his forward rush.

5. Seize his right wrist with your right hand, at the Upper & Lower Wrist Points (H-6 & L-8), and apply stimulation to the Elbow Rub Point (TW-11) with your left forearm.

6. Draw his wrist down and towards your right hip with your right hand, as you stimulate the Elbow Rub Point (TW-11).

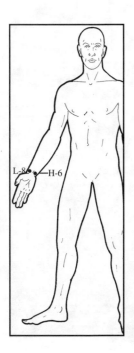

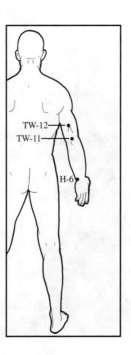

TECHNIQUE # 4 (Cont.)

7-8. The subject is bent over from the reflexive release of his elbow and shoulder. Tap him on the Triceps Hit Point (TW-12) and send him straight to the ground at your feet.

NOTE: As you are performing steps # 5-8, use a strong and commanding voice saying, "FACE DOWN ON THE GROUND! DO IT NOW!"

9. Use both hands to bend the subject's right wrist back. At the same time say, in a command voice, "PUT YOUR HANDS BEHIND YOUR BACK! DON'T RESIST AND YOU WON'T BE HURT!"

10-11. Kneel on his right shoulder with your right knee, and his right hip with your left knee — being careful to stay off his spine — and put him in handcuffs.

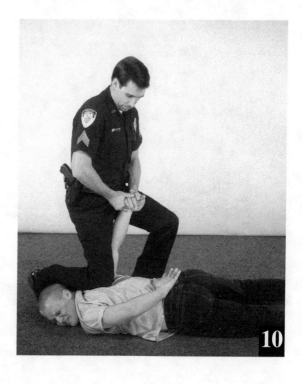

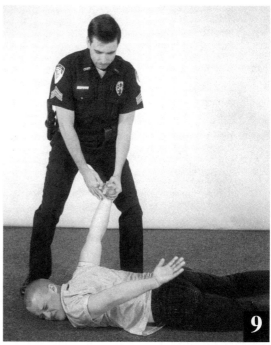

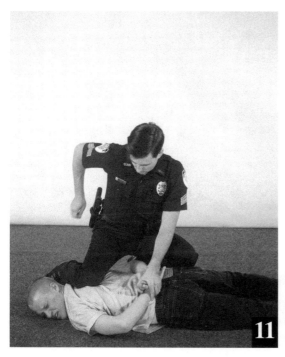

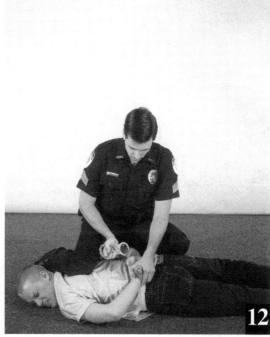

TECHNIQUE # 5
Defense Against a Haymaker

1-2. You are conducting a field interview of a subject, who becomes aggressive, steps towards you with his left foot and throws a wild left haymaker at your head.

3-5. Strike his arm with the knife edge of both your hands. Your right hand hits the Upper Mid-Forearm Point (L-6) while your left hand hits the Outer Forearm Point (LI-10), causing his legs to buckle.

NOTE: Your first move must instantly determine the outcome of the encounter. So, do not block his punch, attack his attack . In about 20% of the populace, just hitting the arm pressure points will be enough to knock the subject to the ground.

6. Grasp his left wrist with your right hand, squeezing on his Upper & Lower Wrist Points (L-8 & H-6).

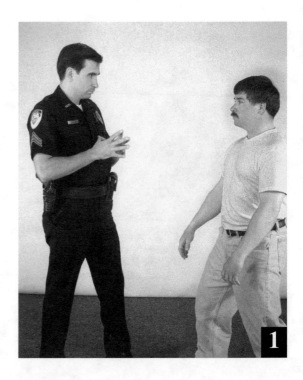

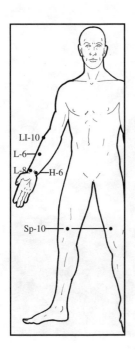

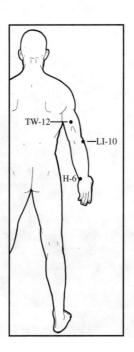

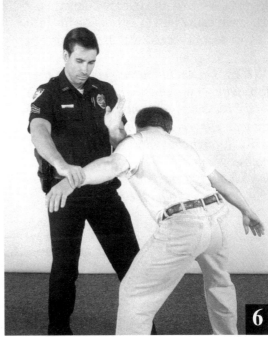

TECHNIQUE # 5 (Cont.)

7. Hold his left shoulder in place with your right hand and strike up with your left knee, hitting him on the upper chest near the shoulder joint.

NOTE: The knee strike need not be very hard. The blow to the upper chest will affect his lungs which have already been affected by the Lung Meridian pressure points you have attacked on his arm.

8-9. Kick him with the toe of your shoe on the Inner Thigh Point (Sp-10) of his right leg.

NOTE: By this step, 90% of all subjects will be knocked to the ground. However, we show the technique continuing in order to reinforce that you are not to stop until the subject has been successfully subdued.

10-11. Strike the subject on the Triceps Hit Point (TW-12) with your left forearm. This will cause him to fall flat on his face at your feet. Proceed with handcuffing.

NOTE: Do not hit the subject's arm too forcefully — you are not trying to break it — the pressure point only requires a modest tap. However, it is important that you strike <u>through</u> the point. Also, take special note of photo # 11 The palm of the subject's hand is turned outward slightly. This makes it easier to hit the point.

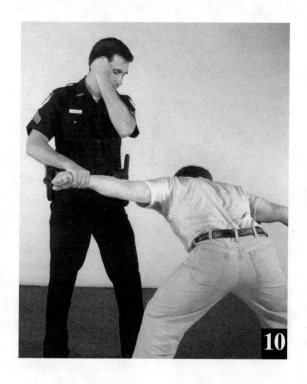

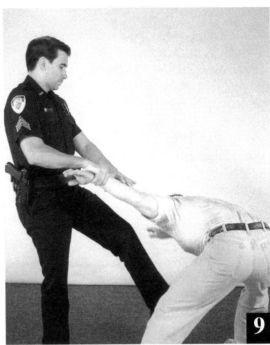

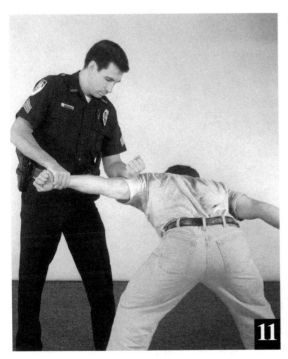

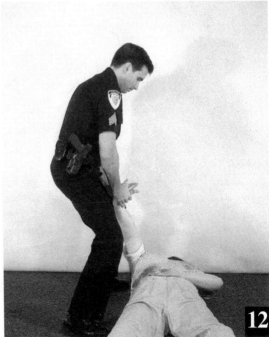

TECHNIQUE # 6
Defense Against a Punch

1-2. You are conducting a field interview of a subject, who becomes suddenly aggressive, stepping towards you with his right foot, reaching with his right hand and winding up to punch you with his left.

3-5. Push his right hand to your right with your left hand and attack the Outer Thigh Point (GB-31) on his right leg with a left snap-kick.

NOTE: When you push his right hand, you are causing his own arm to become an obstruction between you and his intended left punch.

6. Grasp his wrist firmly with your right hand, squeezing on the Upper & Lower Wrist Points (L-8 & H-6).

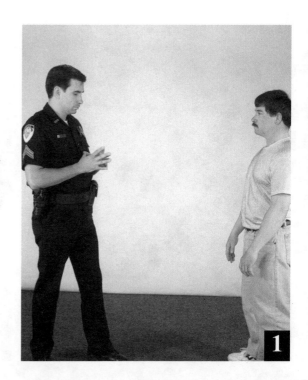

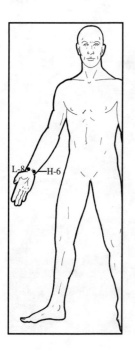

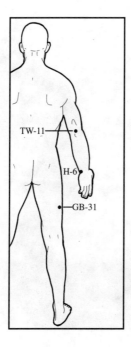

TECHNIQUE # 6 (Cont.)

7-9. Turn his right hand so his palm is facing your body. Using your left forearm manipulate the Elbow Rub Point (TW-11) to put the subject on the ground. Be sure to use a command voice and say, "FACE DOWN ON THE GROUND! DO IT NOW!"

10-12. Use both hands to bend the subject's right wrist back. At the same time say, "PUT YOUR HANDS BEHIND YOUR BACK! DON'T RESIST AND YOU WON'T BE HURT!" Then kneel on his right shoulder with your right knee, his right hip with your left knee, and put him in handcuffs.

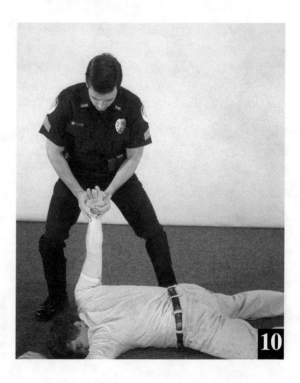

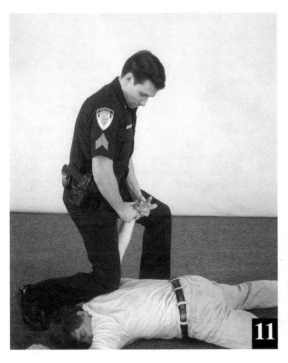
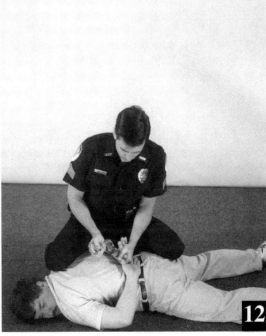

TECHNIQUE # 7
Wrist Grab Defense: Elbow Take-Down

1-2. When subject has grabbed your left wrist with his right hand, move slightly forward and to your left. Bend your elbow and circle your left hand in a clock-wise direction to roll his hand over.

3. Press your left hand forward onto the Lower Mid-Forearm Point (M-UE-28) to loosen his grip. (You are pushing directly towards the subject's sternum.)

4. Bring your right hand up, and cut across the Lower Wrist Point (H-6) as you hold his arm in place with your left hand.

5-6. Grasp firmly, at the Upper & Lower Wrist Points (H-6 & L-8), and turn his palm towards your body as you draw your right hand to your right hip. With your left wrist bone, strike the Elbow Hit Point (TW-12) and send him to the ground.

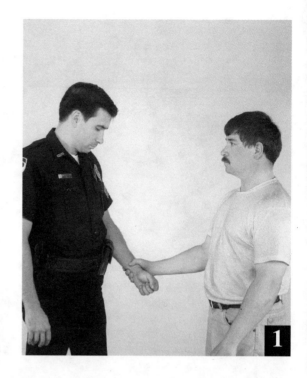

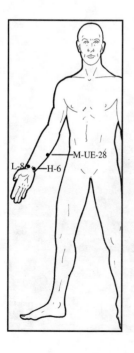

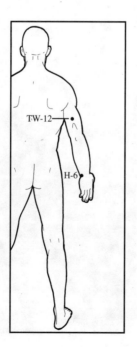

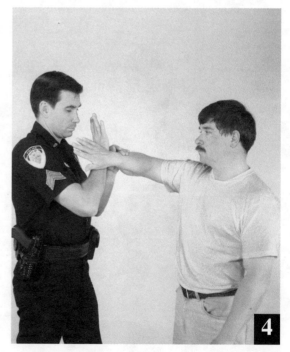

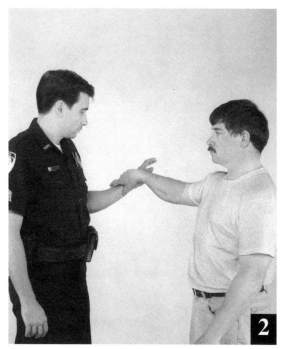

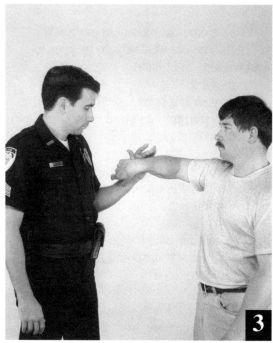

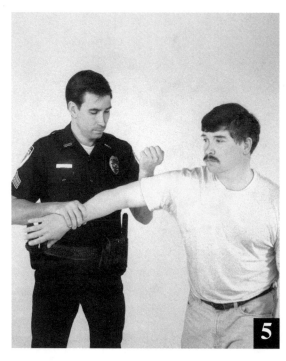

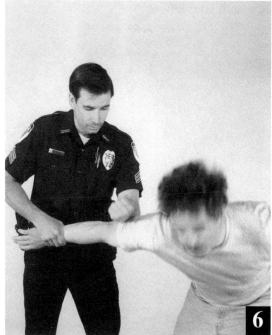

TECHNIQUE # 8
Wrist Grab Defense: Hair Take-Down

1. You are conducting a field interview when the subject suddenly grabs your left arm with his right hand.

2. Draw your left hand to your sternum (into your strength) and turn to the right, pivoting around his grip.

3. With your right hand, grasp the Upper & Lower Wrist Points (L-8 & H-6), and peel your left hand from his grasp.

4. Grab near his elbow with your left hand, and press your thumb into his Outer Forearm Point (LI-10).

5. With your left knee, strike the side of the subject's right leg, hitting the Outer Thigh Point (GB-31).

6. Immediately grasp his hair near his hair-line with your left hand.

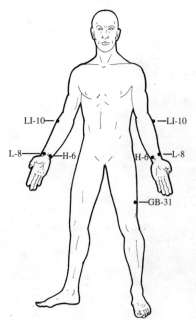

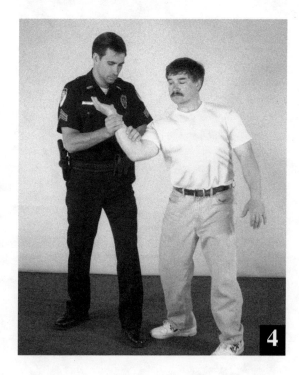

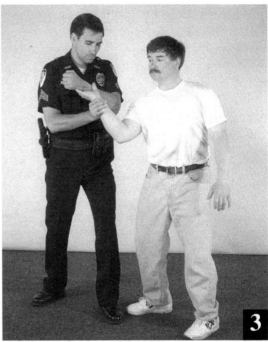

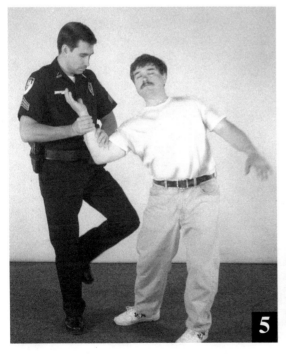

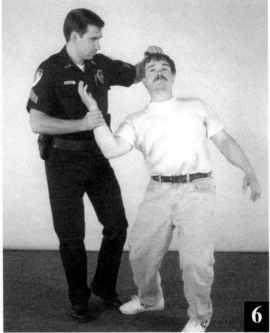

TECHNIQUE # 8 (Cont.)

7-8. Pull His head back as if you are trying to draw his head down to his heels, and throw him to the ground. It is important to throw him so he falls very close to you, right at your feet.

NOTE: Once he is falling to the ground, you must let go of his head, so that his natural reflexes will protect him from hitting it on the ground.

9. Using both hands, bend the subject's wrist (palmar flexion). Put pressure on his wrist by pressing down with your thumbs on the back of his hand, and lifting upward with your fingers on the inside of his wrist (this is called "two-way action").

10-12. Step over the subject and turn his wrist to the right, using the rotation of your body to do this. As you apply this rotation against his bent wrist, he will roll onto his stomach so that you can proceed with handcuffing.

NOTE: As you are performing these steps, use a command voice and say, "FACE DOWN ON THE GROUND! DO IT NOW!"

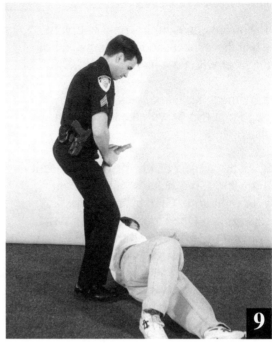

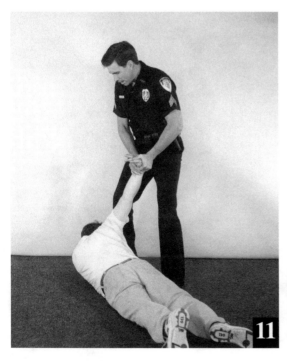
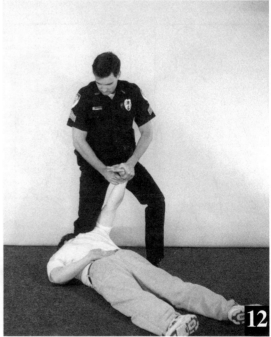

TECHNIQUE # 9
Lapel Grab Defense

1. You are conducting a field interview when the subject suddenly grabs you by the lapel with both hands.

2. Without hesitation, kick to the Lower Leg Point (Sp-6) with the toe of your right shoe.

3. As the subject bends forward in reaction to the blow, reach across his arms with your right arm. Grab his right wrist, squeezing on the Upper & Lower Wrist Points (H-6 & L-8), and trap his left arm against your chest with your forearm.

4. Reach up with your left hand and grab the subject by the hair on the back-left corner of his head.

5-6. Pull his head towards your left hip, turning and unbalancing him.

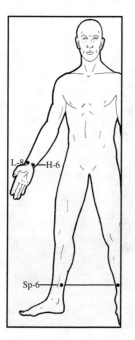
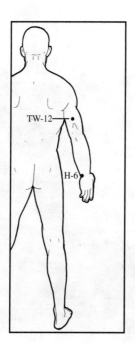

TECHNIQUE # 9 (Cont.)

7-8. Step back with your right leg and turn to your right. At the same time, stretch his right arm and strike the Triceps Hit Point (TW-12) with your left hand to drop the subject to the ground. Be sure to use a command voice and say, "FACE DOWN ON THE GROUND! DO IT NOW!"

NOTE: It would be very easy to continue from step 6 and simply pull the attacker to the ground. However, this action suddenly and completely reverses the direction the subject's body is moving, making it almost impossible for him to offer any resistance.

9-10. Proceed with handcuffing.

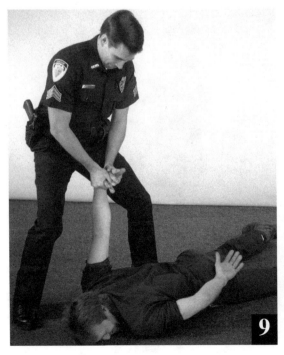

TECHNIQUE # 10
Lapel Grab Defense: Ear Control & Lateral Neck Restraint

1. You are conducting a field interview when the subject suddenly grabs you by the lapel with both hands.

2. Grab his left ear with your right hand, and twist sharply.

3-4. Using the subject's ear for control, roll him into a lateral neck restraint.

NOTE: Check your local jurisdiction's guidelines concerning the use of the lateral neck restraint to insure that you are within policy.

5-6. With your left heel, kick down on the top of his right calf muscle, striking the Leg Stomp Point (B-55) to take his legs out from under him.

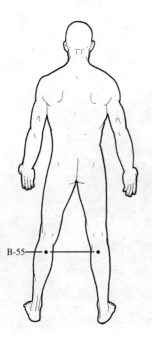

B-55

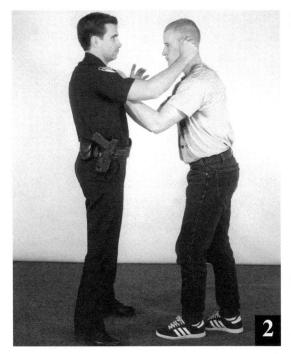
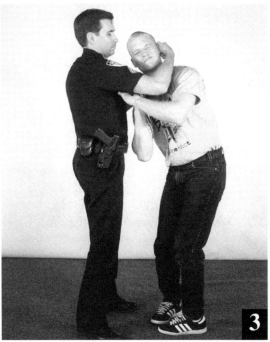

TECHNIQUE # 10 (Cont.)

7. Step back slightly with your left foot and kneel down.

8. Roll to your right bringing the subject into a prone position.

9. Proceed with handcuffing.

NOTE: As you are applying the lateral neck restraint and bringing the attacker to the ground, use a strong and commanding voice, saying, "DON'T RESIST, AND YOU WON'T INJURE YOURSELF!"

Detailed Instruction

A-C. As you grab the subject's ear, grasp it firmly as if you are making a fist. Do not try to hold his ear in your fingertips. And be careful to keep the subject very close to your body.

Keep your forearm away from the subject's mouth to avoid his bite. Secure the lateral neck restraint by anchoring your arm under his jaw (as shown).

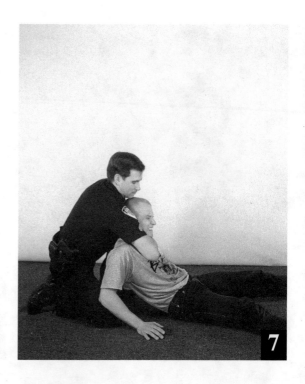

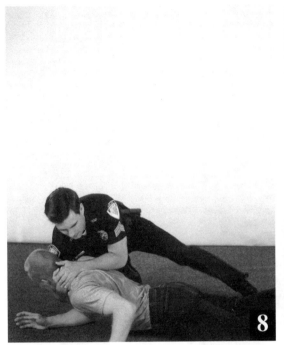

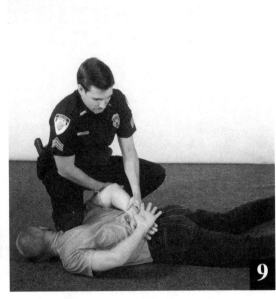

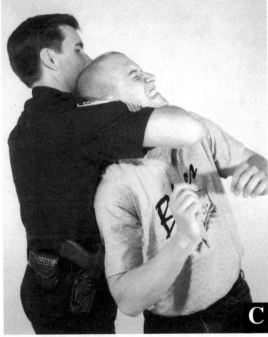

WEAPON CONTROL TECHNIQUES

Because the following techniques illustrate weapon control solutions, a few preliminary comments are in order. In a weapon verses empty-hand situation, the unarmed person will win only against a novice If your opponent is skilled in the use of a particular weapon, you <u>will</u> lose the fight.. For example, as little as thirty minutes training can give a knife-wielding aggressor a huge advantage. As a result, when faced with a weapon, the best defense is to **run**.

In law enforcement situations, there are additional considerations. An armed attacker is a threat not only to the police officer, but also to innocent bystanders. The dictum "protect and serve" requires that police officers place themselves in harm's way and take steps to subdue the armed assailant; however, creating distance is still a preferable course of action. Whenever possible, the officer should retreat, draw his or her sidearm and call for back-up.

It is important to be aware of the distances involved in a weapons encounter. For example, if a suspect has a knife in hand, a police officer must be standing at least 20 feet(!) away in order to have sufficient time to draw, aim and discharge his or her weapon should the suspect suddenly attack. (And, of course, a gun has a significantly greater range than a knife.) This means that at closer distances — especially within the 9 foot Reactionary Gap, and into the Critical Action Interval — retreat is impractical. Therefore, when you are too close to move back — move forward. Charge the attacker and cut off the range of his weapon. Following are some general principles concerning weapon defense.

1. **Never struggle for a weapon.** When an assailant has a weapon, his mind and confidence are in the weapon. If you fight with an attacker for the weapon, you are both mentally preoccupied. Instead, attack the attacker. If the weapon is incidental in your mind, you will see all kinds of openings and targets on your opponent. Use this same mind-set in weapon retention scenarios. When someone grabs for your weapon, most defensive tactics methods teach you to protect your gun by knocking the subject's hand away. Our feeling is to forget about your gun. Instead, lock your attacker's hand to the gun, thereby trapping him helplessly while you subdue him. The object is not to force

him to release your weapon, but instead to make him desperately *want* to let go. If you have him painfully trapped to your gun while yelling, "LET GO OF MY WEAPON, NOW," you will create a psychological panic and confusion in him which will give you a significant strategic advantage

2. **Be aware of others around you.** If you disarm an assailant, there might be someone else nearby who will pick up the weapon and attack you. Always seek to control where the weapon lands.

3. **Keep conscious of the field of fire** when dealing with firearms. If you are struggling with a gun and it discharges, the bullet will hit whatever or whoever is in the way.

4. **Clear the weapon before disarming.** When actually engaging an armed assailant, the most important rule is to "be where the weapon can't hurt you." This means that the first thing to do is either move your body away from the weapon's path, or move the weapon's path away from your body — this is called "clearing the weapon." The second step is to secure the attacker's hand so that he cannot bring the weapon to bear. After this, you may perform the disarm. Sometimes the second step can be omitted and you can simply strike a pressure point to cause the attacker to drop the weapon. However, you must still clear the weapon first so it does not fall towards you. When disarming a subject wielding a firearm, remember that a strike to the Elbow Crease Point (L-5) or the Upper Mid-Forearm Point (L-6) can cause the trigger-finger to flinch, discharging the weapon. This is why we specifically teach the Mid-Forearm Disarm Point (M-UE-28), which does not produce this outcome.

5. **Clear guns to the outside.** When clearing a gun (that is, knocking it aside so that it is not pointing at you) deflect it towards the outside of the attacker's body. Research has demonstrated that a gun is more likely to discharge and wound the defender when the weapon is knocked from the outside inward than when deflected from the inside outward (Taylor & Wanner, 1994).

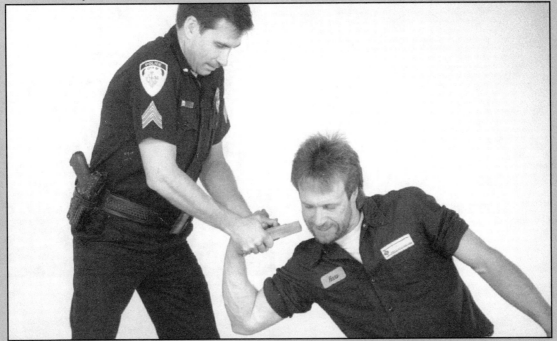

TECHNIQUE # 11
Sidearm Retention: Same Side Grab

1. A subject suddenly grabs your sidearm with his left hand.

2. Pin his hand to your weapon with your right hand, and squeeze into his Upper & Lower Wrist Points (L-8 & H-6).

3-4. Using his wrist as a pivot point, turn to your left to bend his wrist painfully.

NOTE: Lift slightly with your right hand against his bent wrist, causing his elbow to lock and raising him up onto his toes.

5. Slide the subject's left hand off your weapon, and catch one or two of his fingers with your left hand.

6. Lift against the bend of his wrist with your right hand, and bend his fingers down and back with your left hand (see Detailed Instructions on pgs. 210-211).

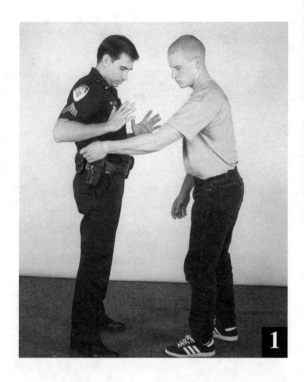

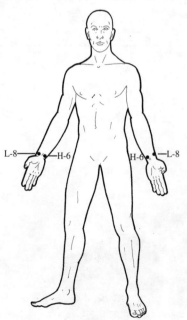

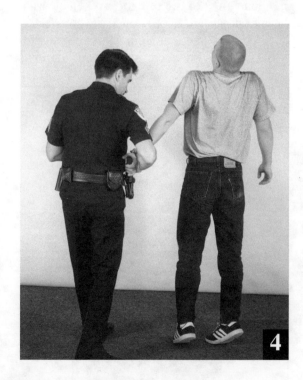

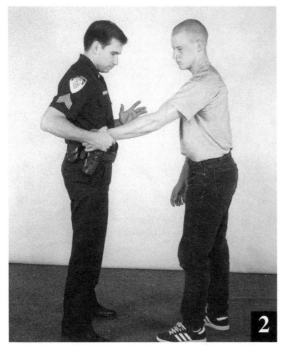

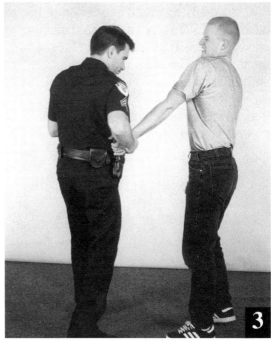

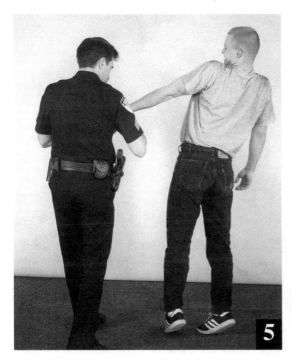

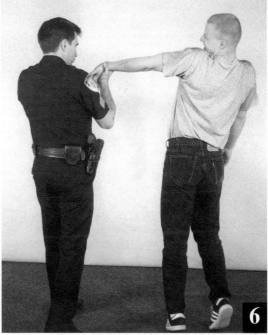

TECHNIQUE # 11 (Cont.)

7-8. Suddenly reverse the direction of his hand so his palm faces downward and use pressure on his fingers to project him to the floor. (In finger control techniques, where the palm faces, the body goes.)

9-12. With the subject face down on the ground, proceed with handcuffing.

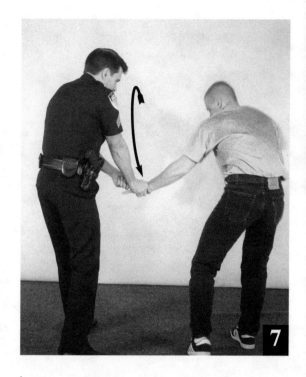

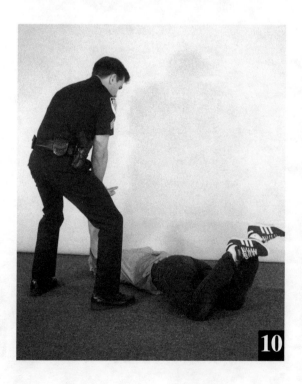

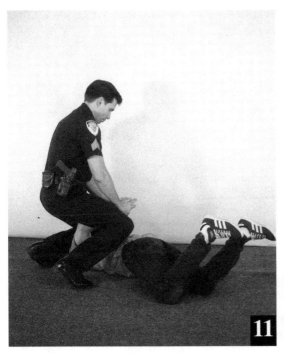

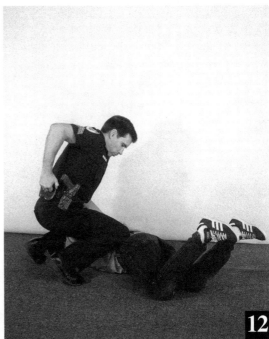

TECHNIQUE # 11
Detailed Instruction

A. When the subject grabs for your gun, do not fight with him over the weapon. Let him have the gun, and use it against him. Concentrate on trapping his hand to your weapon. When you turn, do not try to pull his hand around. Instead, *make his hand the pivot point!*

B. Do not reach for his fingers with your left hand. Instead, position your left hand first, then slide his hand into your waiting grasp.

C. Move your hands in opposing arcs. Your right hand lifts up and towards you, against his wrist, your left hand bends down and away, against his fingers. This creates a tight, circular motion (called "Small Circle") which generates tremendous control and pain with minimum motion.

D. When you reverse direction on his palm, rotate it to your left (counter-clockwise from your perspective). The feeling is similar to cracking a whip.

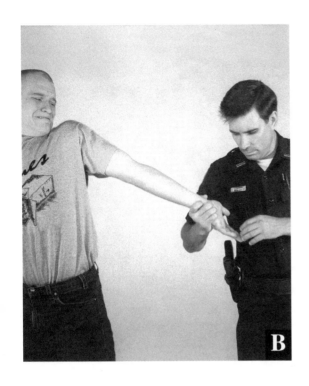

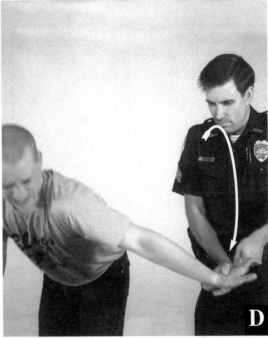

TECHNIQUE # 12
Sidearm Retention: Cross Hand Grab

1. You are conducting a field interview when the subject suddenly reaches across your body with his right hand and grabs for your sidearm.

2-3. Grab his wrist with your right hand, squeezing on the Upper & Lower Wrist Points (L-8 & H-6), and locking his hand against your weapon.

4-6. Turn to your right, stretching the subject's arm, and strike the Triceps Hit Point (TW-12) with your left hand, knocking him to the ground. As you do this, shout, "LET GO OF MY WEAPON, RIGHT NOW!!" Proceed with handcuffing, or disengage and draw your weapon while back-up arrives.

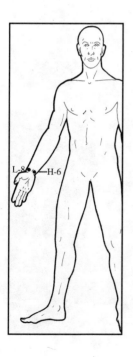
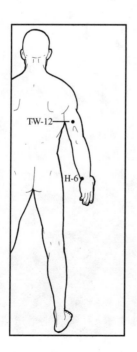

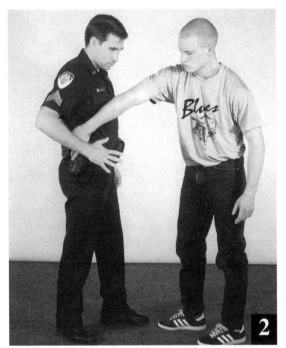

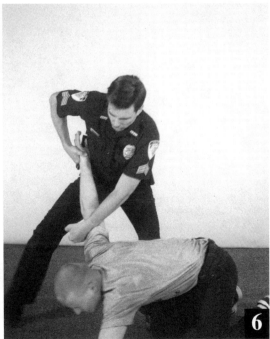

TECHNIQUE # 13
Sidearm Retention: Rear Grab

1. A subject has snuck up behind you, and grabbed your sidearm with his right hand.

2. Grab his hand with your right hand, pinning it to the butt of your gun. Lock your arm tightly, trapping his arm to your body, with your elbow pressed up against his Elbow Rub Point (TW-11).

3-4. Turn to your right, using his trapped hand as a pivot point. The pressure on his wrist and elbow will cause him to move to the left. Keep him moving by turning to your right.

5. Reach up with your left hand, peel his hand from your weapon and bend his wrist back as you send him to the ground.

6. Pin the subject to the ground with your right knee, as you begin handcuffing.

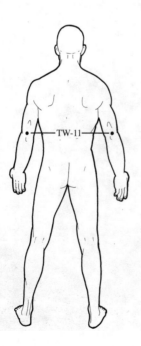

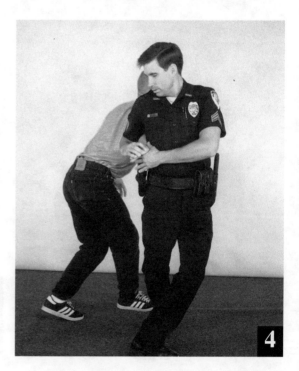

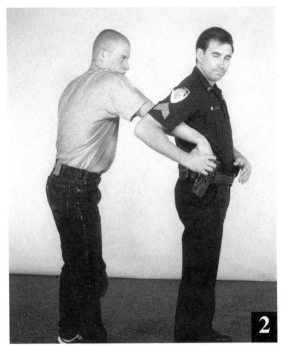
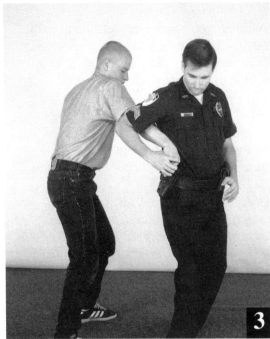

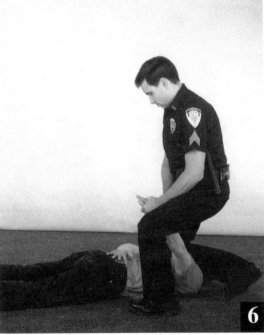

TECHNIQUE # 13
Detailed instruction

A-B. As you pin the subject's hand to the butt of your gun, it is important to squeeze your arm tightly. This insures that he is unable to pull away.

C. As you rotate to the right, applying pressure to his wrist and elbow, his left arm will swing away from you. This means that he cannot use it to attack you.

D. As his body moves, his hand will loosen its grip on your weapon and his wrist will bend over, ready for you to apply pressure for handcuffing control. You create mental confusion by yelling, "LET GO OF THE WEAPON." He will be eager to do just that, but unable to comply until you are ready.

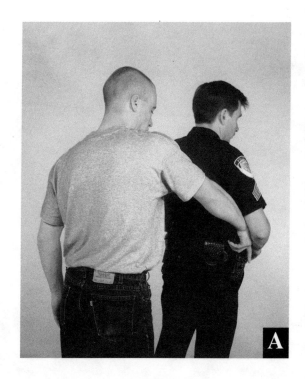

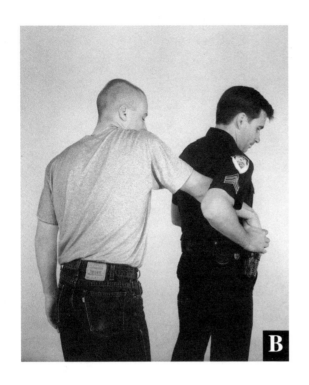

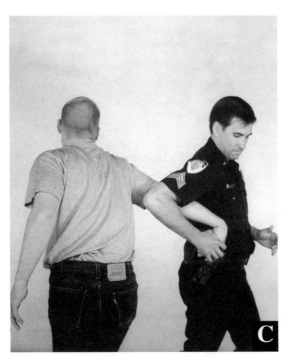

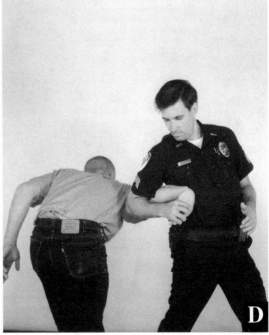

TECHNIQUE # 14
Weapon Retention: Barrel Seizure

1. You have your weapon drawn and leveled at a suspect. However, you are much too close for safety.

2. Before you can create a safe distance between yourself and the suspect, he reaches up with his right hand and grasps your gun from underneath by the barrel.

3-4. Place your left hand on top of his fingers, pinning him to the gun. Press down with your left hand, driving the barrel into the web of the suspect's right hand.

5-6. Chop his right biceps with your left hand, as you pull your gun towards your right hip (see detailed instruction on the following pages). At the same time, slide backward to create a safe distance between yourself and the suspect.

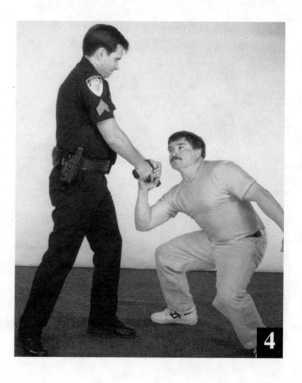

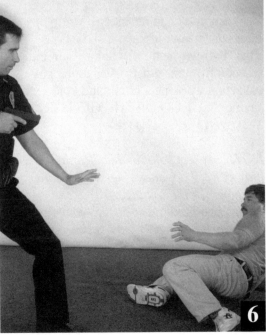

TECHNIQUE # 14
Detailed Instruction

A-B. When you press down on the suspect's fingers, you should pull back slightly with your left hand at the base of the pistol grip. This will create a small circle movement of the gun which overcomes his grip. Once his control is compromised, push the gun towards him. The untrained reflex would be to wrestle for the gun and try to pull it away. This solution involves giving the gun to the suspect by pushing it at him.

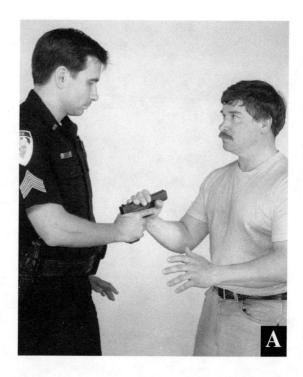

NOTE: When a suspect grabs your gun, the use of deadly force is justified. With your hand on his fingers, you have sufficient leverage to aim the gun directly at his chest. If you fire at the subject, your hand will be protected from the action of the slide by his hand. Though this solution affords you the deadly force option, we advocate the humane outcome.

C. When you chop his biceps, you pull your gun to your hip at the same time. This "two-way action" will easily free the weapon from his grasp. Add to the physical action by using a command voice and saying, "LET GO OF THE GUN OR YOU WILL BE SHOT!!"

NOTE: At any point in this technique, you may kick the opponent's left leg at either the Inner Thigh Point (Sp-10) or the Lower Leg Point (Sp-6) using your right foot. Such a move will break down the subject's resistance to your technique, and will keep you from becoming preoccupied with your gun.

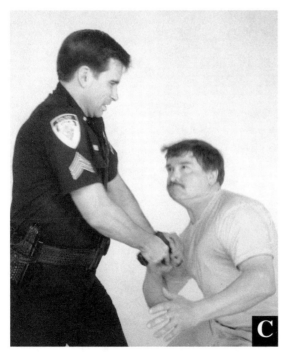

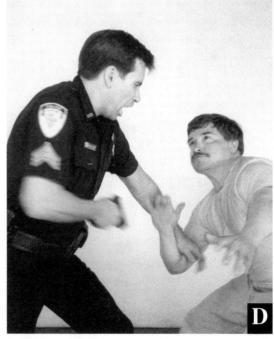

TECHNIQUE # 15
Weapon retention: Two Handed Seizure

1. You have your weapon drawn and leveled at a suspect. However, you are much too close for safety.

2. Before you can create a safe distance between yourself and the suspect, he grasps the barrel of the gun with his right hand, and your wrist with his left hand.

3. Because you choose not to shoot the subject, you grab his hand with your left hand, pinning him to the barrel of your weapon.

4-5. Slide forward with your left foot, and drive the gun into the Inguinal Crease Points (Sp-12 & Li-12) at the top of the subject's right leg.

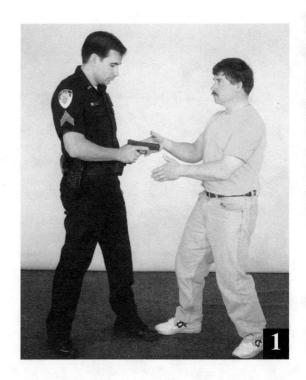

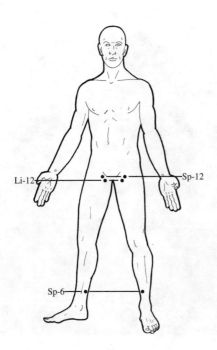

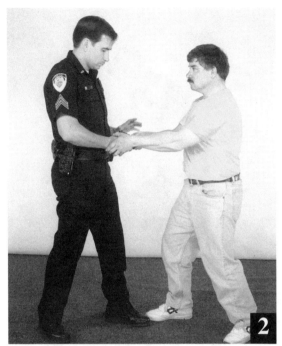

TECHNIQUE # 15 (Cont.)

6. Stomp across the Lower Leg Point (Sp-6) of the subject's right leg with your right foot, to drive him to the ground.

7. As he falls, use your left hand to drive his hands away, as you pull your weapon towards your right hip.

8. Slide away to create distance between yourself and the subject.

Detailed Instruction

A-B. When the subject grabs your weapon, you do not pull away, or try to knock his hands off. Instead, you trap his hands to the gun and push it towards him. This approach is the opposite of what he would expect, and unbalances him both physically and psychologically. As you are trapping his hand to your weapon increase his disorientation by yelling, "LET GO OF THE GUN OR YOU WILL BE SHOT."

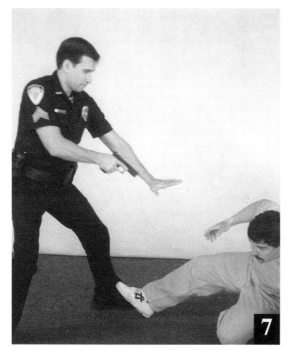

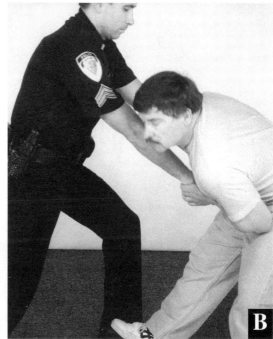

TECHNIQUE # 16
Gun Disarm I

1. A subject holds a pistol against your chest.

2. With your left hand, clear the gun to your left side, being mindful of what is in the field of fire.

3-4. Swing your right forearm against the Mid-Forearm Disarm Point (M-UE-28) on the subject's right arm, causing his wrist to bend and the weapon to drop.

5-6. Step to the left and pivot to the right as you bend and twist his wrist back to drive him face down to the ground, all the while saying, "ON THE GROUND! DO IT NOW AND YOU WON'T BE HURT."

NOTE: As you drop him down, apply a twisting motion against his bent wrist to project him forward, away from the gun.

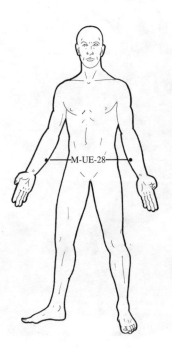

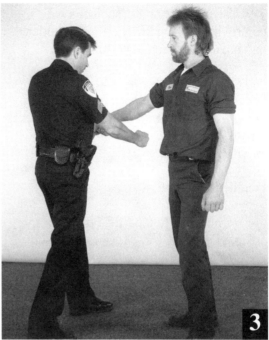

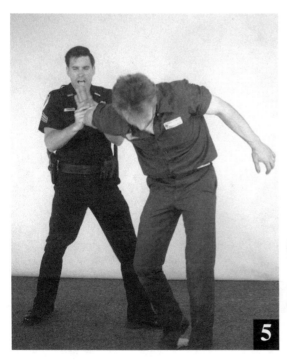

TECHNIQUE # 16 (Cont)

7-9. Use pressure on the subject's wrist to control him as you kneel on his shoulder and hip and proceed to cuff him.

NOTE: In this technique you have controlled where the gun has landed so that you are able to keep it in sight at all times. This is important in the event that other people are present.

Detailed Instruction

A-C. The strike to the Mid-Forearm Disarm Point (M-UE-28) causes the subject's wrist and elbow to bend. This gives you tremendous control and numerous options for follow-up.

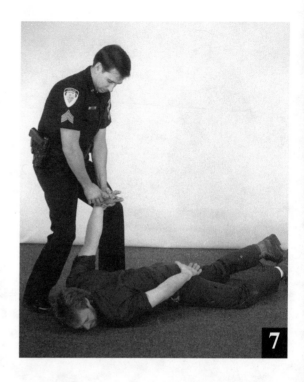

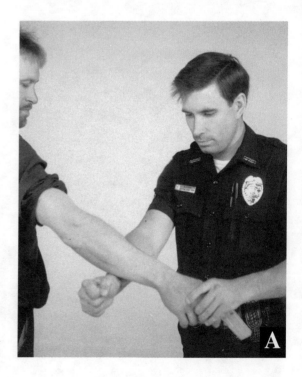

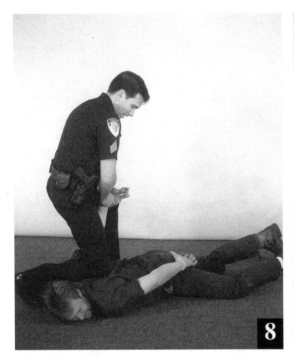

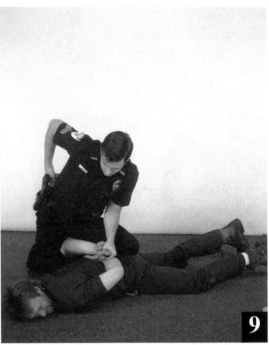

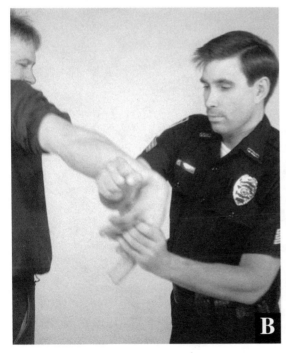

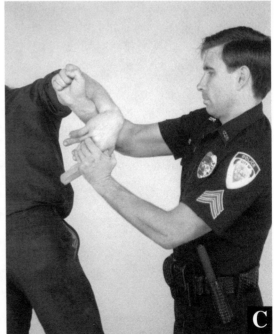

TECHNIQUE # 17
Gun Disarm II

1. A subject has pointed a handgun at your face. Your hands are raised in apparent submission.

2. Clear the weapon to your left side with your right hand, grasping firmly over his thumb.

NOTE: At this moment, the gun is pointed to your left. Be aware of bystanders who might be in the field of fire.

3. Reach up with your left hand and grab butt of the weapon, pinning his little finger with the palm of your hand.

NOTE: Between steps 3 & 4 it can be helpful to kick the subject's left leg — at either the Inner Thigh Point (Sp-10) or the Lower Leg Point (Sp-6) — with your right foot.

4-6. Bend his wrist back and rotate it left to right, bringing the barrel of the gun to bear on the subject's own face.

NOTE: The combination of bend and twist will bring the subject to his knees. At the same time, his left hand will swing back and away, a reaction called the "crossed extensor reflex."

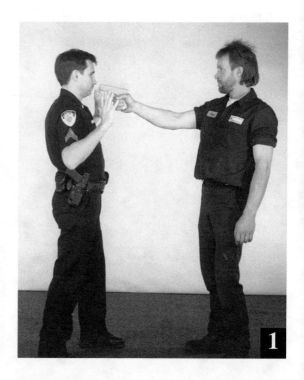

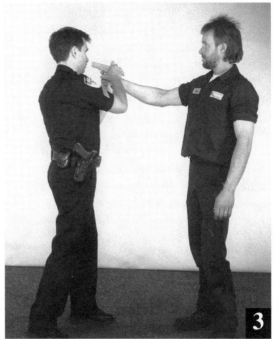

TECHNIQUE # 17 (Cont.)

7-9. Pivot to your right and twist the subject's hand to the right. This will project him face down to the ground. At the same time, use your command voice saying, "DROP THE GUN! DO IT NOW AND YOU WON'T BE HURT!"

NOTE: You are commanding the subject to drop his gun, something he cannot do because you are literally holding his hand to the weapon. This creates a high level of psychological distress in the subject, which helps to break down his resistance.

10-12. Pull the gun from his grasp and move it out of reach. Then reverse the bend on his wrist as you kneel on his shoulder and hip to cuff.

NOTE: Reversing the bend of his wrist (from dorsal flexion to palmar flexion) causes a great amount of disorientation and pain.

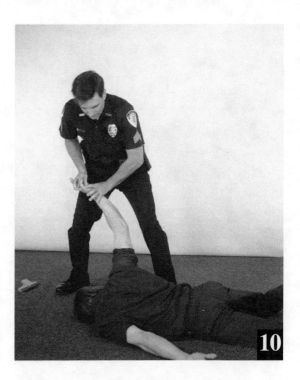

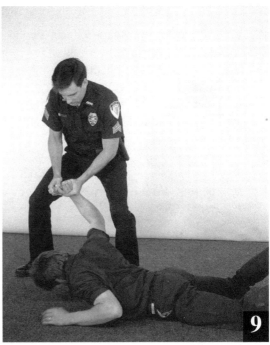

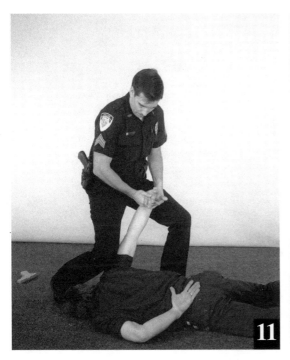

TECHNIQUE # 17
Detailed Instruction

A. When you clear the weapon, clear to the outside. Do not clear the weapon by using your left hand and pushing his arm to your right. Pressure on the back of his hand can cause his finger to tighten on the trigger, increasing the likelihood that you will be shot.

As you are clearing the weapon to your left, you must move your left hand out of the field of fire. Pull it in to your chest, or down tightly to your side (as shown in photo A).

When you grab his hand, do not grab his wrist or forearm. If you do, he will still be able to point the gun at you simply by bending his wrist. If the subject is holding a 9mm automatic, be careful to secure the slide tightly. If he fires the weapon, your grip on the slide will prevent a fresh round from chambering. If your grip is weak, the action of the slide could injure your hand.

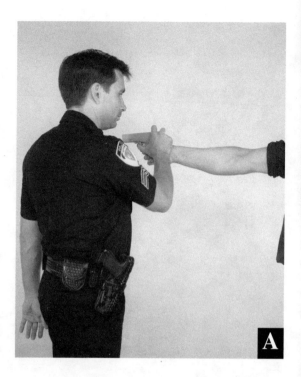

B. When you grasp with both hands it is important that you wrap your fingers firmly around his grip so that he feels trapped against his own gun. You must secure his hand in yours so that he cannot pull away and shoot you.

C-D. The key to manipulating the wrist is to bend and turn at the same time. Apply pressure against his little finger by pushing with the palm of your left hand. In this motion you will be applying two-way and even three-way action as you push his fingers back, pull his wrist towards you and rotate his hand inward.

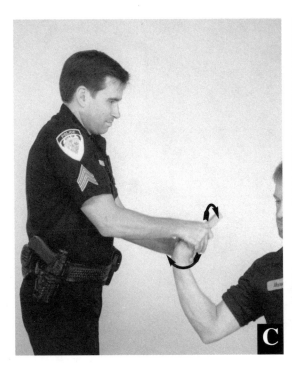

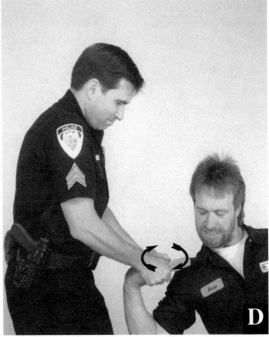

CONCLUSION

We cannot stress enough the importance of willingness and commitment in self-defense. If you are ready and willing to do anything it takes to defend yourself, then and only then will you be in a position to restrain your actions and fight humanely. Until you are convinced that protecting your own life is far more important than not injuring your attacker, you will not have the confidence and determination necessary to perform humane self-protection.

In every case, you must be prepared to go beyond the techniques we have shown and use more ruthless methods if necessary. Such a willingness will enable you to commit fully to all your techniques, and will cause your humane tactics to work more effectively.

We also want to stress the fact that reading a book is not enough to develop self-defense skills. You must ingrain the techniques into your body by actually practicing what you find in these pages. And, we do recommend that your practice be supervised by a qualified instructor of *Humane Pressure Point Self-Defense*.

LEFT: Leon Jay, Ernie Reyes, Sr., George Dillman. Dillman was the special guest lecturer for the 2000 World Association Mastery Team Instructor's Camp, headed by Reyes. Reyes is a well known martial artist and actor who was featured in the action-comedy, *Surf Ninjas.*

BELOW: George Dillman, Allen Dillman, and Bill "Superfoot" Wallace.

"Dillman knows the musculo-skeletal system better than some doctors."

Ralph Buschbacher, M.D.
Indianapolis, IN

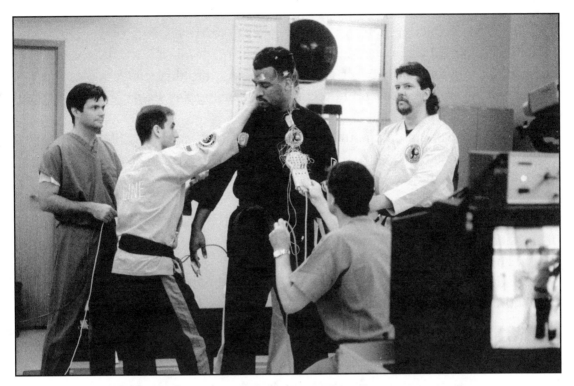

PRESSURE POINT TECHNIQUES: HOW SAFE ARE THEY?
*A Team of Doctors Tries to Find Out**

George Dillman has been actively teaching pressure point techniques to martial artists, police officers and others since 1983. Throughout, Dillman has maintained that pressure point techniques are an effective and humane form of self-defense. That the techniques are effective has been ably demonstrated by the fact that Dillman and his students routinely perform pressure point knock outs as part of the teaching and learning process.

People knocked out using pressure point techniques are fine after they have been revived. This, Dillman insists, shows that pressure point fighting is actually a humane method of self-defense, because it renders an assailant unconscious without causing damage. But, how can anyone say for certain that no harm is caused?

In 1997, a team of scientists in Philadelphia, Pennsylvania, USA, using state-of-the-art bio-medical monitoring equipment, collected data on 17 pres-

---

* Portions of the text and photographs in this Appendix have been previously published in Black Belt Magazine (USA), September, 1998 ["Pressure Point Techniques: A Team of Doctors Tries to Find Out How Safe They Are," by Chris Thomas], and in Martial Arts Illustrated (England), October, 1999, Vol. 12, No. 5 ["Is Safe Pressure Point Practice Possible?" by Chris Thomas].

sure point knock outs in an effort to examine the relative safety of the Dillman Method. As one of them stated, "From a scientific point of view, it is very interesting to understand what is going on. Going into this study, one of our concerns was: are [pressure point techniques] causing any damage to the people who are getting knocked out?"

However, one point should be clearly stated: It is impossible to conclusively prove a negative, especially when dealing with systems as complex as the human body. In other words, scientists can never "prove beyond a shadow of a doubt" that pressure point techniques cause no harm. All they can do is look for evidence of harm. In the absence of such evidence, the relative safety of the techniques can be reasonably presumed.

The scientists involved were Mark Stecker, M.D., a Neurologist and team leader; Charles Terry, M.D., a Physiatrist and member of Dillman Karate International; Terry Patterson, Ph.D., a Neuro-physiologist; Michelle Murphy, an EEG (Electro-Encephalogram) Technologist; and research assistant David Barclay.

The study participants included, George Dillman, Kim Dillman, Ron Richards, Bill Hatt, Avish Parashar, Mike Worth, all from Pennsylvania; Evan Pantazi of Massachusetts; Bill Burch and Tom Cameron from Illinois; Ed Lake, and John Ralston from Florida; Mark Kline, Arthur Hearns, Brandon Ayres, Todd Quan, and Jack Hugate, from New Jersey; John Westover from New Hampshire; Steve Downs and Jeff Skorupski from Maine. In addition to the participants, there were other martial artists who came to assist and observe.

Subjects to be knocked out were wired to EEG, which monitors brainwaves, ECG (electrocardiogram) for recording heart rhythms, a sphygmomanometer to take blood pressure readings, and a fingertip Pulse/Oxygen meter, which provides information on pulse rate and oxygen saturation of the blood.

Tests of cognitive impairment were also performed. Each subject was told two words as he was collapsing from the pressure point strike. After revival, he was asked to repeat the two words. He was also asked questions to determine his orientation, such as his name, the date, how to spell "world" backwards and so forth.

"The question is, what's the mechanism here?" Explained Dr. Patterson. "Physiologically, what is it that happens? To the best of my knowledge, no one knows. Does the blood pressure drop to zero? Does the EEG flatten out? Do you get massive pupil constriction or dilation? These are unknown. No one's ever looked at it."

For the first sample, George Dillman performed a "kidney knock out". This technique involves "setting up" the kidney with a strike to a point on the triple warmer (san jiao) meridian of the arm. Then, the back is slapped at the kidney "associated" and "alarm" points which lie a hand-width apart on the Gall Bladder and Bladder meridians respectively.

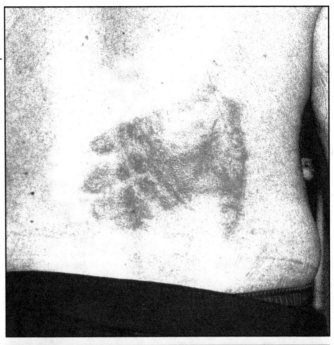

As Dillman struck, the subject stiffened up and dropped flat on his face like a falling tree. This dramatic knock out caused the scientists great concern, and they were quite relieved when they saw that the "post event" EEG and ECG readings were normal. This was an important preliminary result, because if the doctors had identified anything which was a clear evidence of harm, the study could not have proceeded any further.

This "kidney knock out" is one of the few pressure point maneuvers to leave a mark.

This computer enhanced photo shows the details of the palm print left after the performance of the "kidney knock out." The blow itself was not strong enough to account for the reaction of the skin, especially through the heavy fabric of the subject's karate uniform. George Dillman believes this phenomenon resulted from the transfer of internal energy, or "chi."

After revival, the subject's uniform top was removed, revealing a clearly defined hand print at the point of impact. The hand print — which included palm lines and was surrounded by an area of reddened and raised flesh — resembled the aural images recorded with Kirlian photography. In many ways, the mark looked like it was caused by heat, rather than impact, a fact that drew some surprised comments from the researchers.

The first sample immediately revealed the problems which would plague the research. The signals — in particular the EEG signals — were partially obscured by artifact. Artifact might be compared with static on a television set. It arose from two main sources. The first was the jiggling of the EEG leads attached to the scalp as the subject was struck and fell.

The second source of artifact was muscular tension. EEG measures very small electrical signals from the brain. During the moment of impact, muscles in the subject's face would sometimes tighten up. Because electrical signals

MEDICAL TESTING

1. A test subject grabs Ed Lake by the lapels to simulate an attack. This is done because the act of grabbing tightens muscle groups and creates vulnerability in the pressure points Lake uses.

2. Lake strikes diagonally downward against the acupuncture points Stomach # 25, located on either side of the naval.

3-4 The subject collapses unconscious into the arms of the catcher.

5-6. The doctors examine the subject as he revives from the blow.

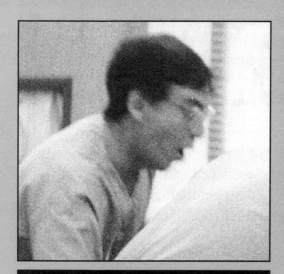

Most of the medical researchers were seeing pressure point techniques for the first time. They were clearly impressed by what they witnessed.

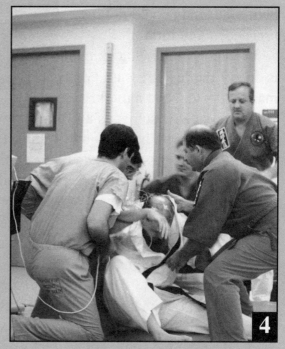

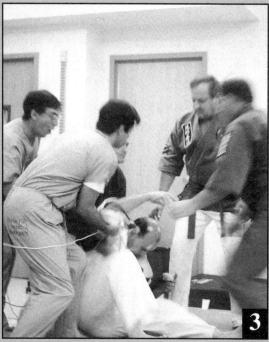

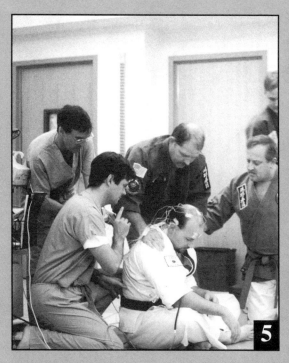

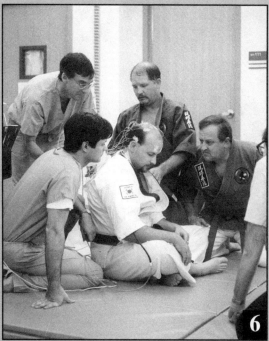

from muscular tension are generally more intense than signals from the brain, they tended to "drown out" the brain signals.

Extensive computer processing of the signal has the ability to filter out some of this artifact. But, it was important to reduce this effect as much as possible. So, as the testing progressed, helpers worked hard to catch and carefully lower subjects in order to minimize the problem. It was also necessary to delay the revival process for several seconds.

In a pressure point demonstration an unconscious or stunned volunteer is immediately revived with a light slap and massage along the back of the neck. (In western medical terms, this stimulates the spinal accessory nerve. In oriental medical terms, this restores the yang-chi to the head by stimulating the Gall Bladder meridian.) This process itself was interesting to the scientists. As Dr. Terry noted, "We are finding fascinating correlations [between pressure point revival methods and] things that you do to comatose patients just to see if you can find any responses. It would be great to find a therapeutic application [for pressure points] as well."

Chris Thomas, Chas Terry, M.D., Kim Dillman, George Dillman, Michelle Murphy, and David Barclay during medical research into pressure point techniques.

Unfortunately, the revival process was producing more artifact. So, at the request of the doctors, subjects were simply lowered as readings were recorded. Then, only after the doctors had obtained sufficient data (which, thankfully, took less than twenty seconds), was the revival performed.

As would be expected, different individuals responded differently to the light application of pressure point techniques. Some appeared only slightly dazed or disoriented after the 'event.' Others were completely limp and unresponsive. Interestingly, however, the level of perceived consciousness and the level of disorientation did not always coincide.

For example, one subject, who never appeared to lose consciousness, was completely unaware of the two memory words spoken to him. He was unable to spell "world" either backwards or forwards and was generally confused. Another subject, who collapsed like a rag-doll and remained completely limp and unmoving until the revival had been administered, heard and easily repeated the two words, as well as successfully completing the other cognitive tasks (even though he described himself as feeling dazed and light-headed).

The subjects showed signs of stress during the research. As a group, being mostly younger and in good health, they should have shown average or below average blood pressures. However, prior to receiving the knock out techniques, the subjects virtually all had blood pressures significantly higher than normal. This was clearly a response to the anxiety of waiting to be struck. Dr. Stecker wondered if this state of higher blood pressure and elevated adrenaline might in some ways resemble the heightened state of arousal an attacker would have in a self-defense encounter.

As the testing progressed, the doctors were relieved and surprised that they were not finding the potentially harmful outcomes they had considered possible. Dr. Patterson described one of the anticipated results, a sudden slowing of the heart.

"If you're looking for a dramatic heart rate response, swim along the top of the pool, take a normal breath and [do a surface] dive, you'll get a massive bradycardia. The heart rate drops right out. It will become amazingly low, and it will stay there for a while, step back up, overshoot a little, drop back down and come back up again. I was expecting to see at least that sort of bradycardic effect."

In fact there seemed to be no particular trend in terms of physiological response to the application of pressure point techniques. For example, the heart-rate of the subject of the "kidney knock out" showed an upward trend. A knock out performed on the Gallbladder meridian produced a downward trend

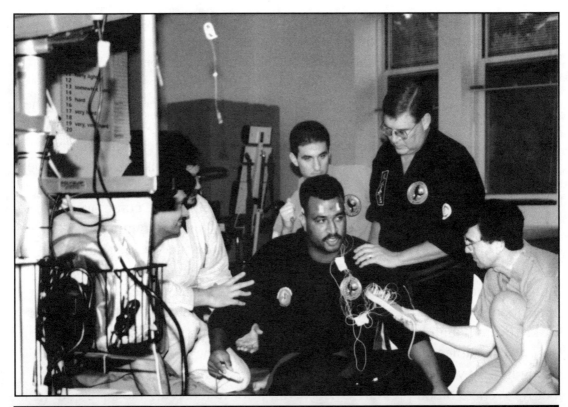

Researchers examine a subject following a pressure point knock out to determine the degree of cognitive and neurological impairment caused by pressure point techniques. Subjects recovered quickly after being knocked out, and the researchers did not find any evidence that they were harmed. This research supports the claim that pressure point methods represent a humane option for self-defense.

in heart-rate, and a knock out performed on Stomach point # 9 (a point associated with the carotid sinus) produced no change in heart rate.

Dr. Stecker was intrigued by what was not happening. "We know it's not a seizure. We know it's not cardiac arrest — at least not for a long period of time. We know that the blood does not desaturate," he said. "Whatever it is, it's incontrovertible that it does something to the person. You can't miss that."

But, he was not at all bothered by this. In fact, he seemed quite pleased. "It turns out that if we find nothing, that's the most exciting thing of all, because then it's something that we don't yet have a good explanation for. If it stops the heart — big deal — we understand that. But if it's something completely different, it would be nice to understand what that was. The best part is to learn something new."

Dr. Patterson, who has a background in karate seemed quite impressed by the techniques he witnessed. "Very, very interesting," he said. "I studied Shotokan karate many years ago, and reached first dan (though I have been inactive for some time now, unfortunately). This stuff no one was allowed to know about. You didn't even know it existed until you hit second or third dan."

As the day progressed, the scientists began to ask about the possibility of having the subject either lying down or seated during the knock outs. Though this is not common in pressure point practice, the last two volunteers were knocked out while seated. As each collapsed, they were cradled in the arms of a "catcher" while data was collected. This method produced clear measurements with minimal affect. Because each of these last two subjects had been knocked out at the beginning of the day, it also provided an indication as to any cumulative effects of these techniques.

Even before the study was over, Dr. Stecker was thinking about how future studies might be designed — wondering how neuro-inhibitors, Beta-blockers or narcotic antagonists might alter the effect of the techniques, and provide clues as to the underlying mechanisms.

But, for this first scientific look at pressure point methods, the most important question was, Are these techniques dangerous? "This was a pilot study. The data we collected provides us with possible directions for future research," said Dr. Terry. "But this much we can say: we did not find any conclusive evidence to suggest that the subjects are harmed."

This conclusion was echoed in a scientific paper presenting the results of the research. In it the doctors wrote, "Although we have not demonstrated that pressure point techniques are generally safe, no hazardous complications were demonstrated and no immediately dangerous phenomena such as arrhythmias, hypotension, desaturation, or seizures were noted."[*]

This is the cautious scientists' way of saying that they found nothing which would support the claim that the moderate application of pressure point techniques poses a threat to either a seminar volunteer or an attacker. However, such a statement is not an endorsement for recklessly performing pressure point techniques on people.

Though it is scientifically impossible to "prove" a negative, and an initial study such as this one is highly limited in scope, these findings do provide credible, objective evidence to support Dillman's statement that Pressure Point Self-Defense is a safe and humane method.

---

[*] Terry, Charles, MD; Barclay, David; Patterson, Terry, PhD; Stecker, Mark; MD. Physiologic study of pressure point techniques used in martial arts. J. Sports Med Phys Fitness 1999; 39: 328-35

KNOCK OUTS WITH THE SUB-JECT SEATED

During the medical research, one on-going problem was caused by artifact. Artifact is signal interference — like static on a television — which makes it difficult to monitor a subject's physio-logical state. Much of the artifact was caused by movement and jiggling of the wires attached to the subject as he fell to the ground. To minimize this prob-lem, the last two subjects where knocked out while sitting Japanese-style on the floor. As they collapsed, they were cradled by "catchers" as readings were recorded.

1. Test subject Bill Burch grabs Kim Dillman by the lapel to simulate an attack.

2. Dillman strikes Burch on both Jaw Stun Points (S-5), knocking him uncon-scious.

3. Unconscious, Burch is cradled by helpers as his physiological condition is monitored.

4. As he revives, Burch is tested to determine his level of cognitive impair-ment.

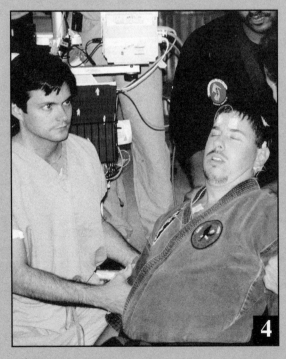

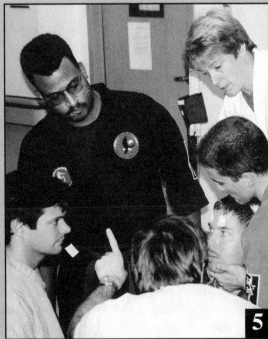

"Dillman's theories have changed the way I practice."

Charles Joseph Swift
Japan

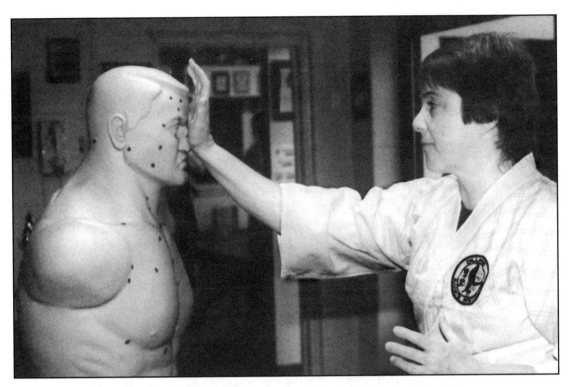

FROM THE BOOK TO THE STREET
Training Methods of
Humane Pressure Point Self-Defense

Sometimes, in moments of crisis, a person is saved by suddenly remembering something read or heard. This means it is possible that you could find yourself
responding correctly when attacked simply because you have read this book.
However, it is best not to count on reading to be enough. Interpersonal violence creates a level of psychological stress far more intense than other types of crises. In
order to prepare yourself to face such an encounter, you must utilize practice methods
designed to effectively condition your mind and body for appropriate response. The
most effective training methods are those conducted by an instructor skilled in
Humane Pressure Point Self-Defense. However, we are including some exercises
which you can do on your own to increase your readiness to face violence.

MENTAL TRAINING

Mental training is about seeing the world through new eyes. The world does
not change, but your viewpoint does. For example, when someone reaches out to grab
the average individual the reaction is, "Oh no, he's grabbing me. What shall I do?"
However, when a pressure point expert is grabbed the reaction is, "Oh good, he's
grabbing me. Look at all the pressure points he is exposing. I'll just take my pick."
To begin to cultivate this kind of mind-set, simply look for pressure points and vital

targets whenever you are people-watching. Mentally look for the points and targets we have presented here, and you will begin to see people as a mix of strengths and weaknesses. This is a healthier view of people anyway (since we all have strengths and weaknesses, physically, mentally, emotionally and spiritually), and it will enable you to feel less as if you are weak and helpless, while others are strong and dangerous.

The samurai of feudal Japan understood that the greatest impediment to the warrior was the fear of death. Using the philosophy of Zen-buddhism as their guide, they cultivated the qualities of detachment from life and acceptance of death. While their approach is too extreme for our purposes, their insight still applies. What prevents most people from defending themselves is the fear of being hurt. Ironically, this fear causes people to freeze up and fail to fight back when they should — when it could make a difference — and they end up getting hurt. The attitude which will protect you is to accept that you <u>will</u> be hurt. Then, having accepted injury as a foregone conclusion, you can concentrate on fighting back and making the attacker pay a cost for everything he does to you. As we have mentioned, just this attitude is often enough to dissuade a predator.

In order to cultivate this mind-set, begin by imagining a situation in which someone you love is being assaulted. Allow yourself to picture this vividly, and feel the rise of anger and rage within you. With that anger as your fuel, picture yourself defeating the assailant and saving your loved one using the humane tactics we have described. Repeat this exercise several times, sometimes viewing it from the perspective of an observer — like watching a movie — sometimes seeing it through your own eyes. Also, seek to include vivid details like color and sound.

Once you have "gotten in touch with your anger" picture a new scenario where you are the one being attacked. In the same way, envision yourself successfully defending against the attack. Be careful to have the same sense of outrage and anger fueling your imaginary self-defense as you had fueling your imaginary defense of a loved one.

THE GLARE

Anger can be an emotion that leads to uncontrollable outbursts; but anger can also be a powerful fuel that drives us to protect ourselves and others. Sometimes the distinction is made between "hot" anger and "cold" anger. Hot anger is out of control. In a fight situation, a person in the grips of hot anger will flail wildly, lashing out without any apparent awareness of what is really going on around them. Hot anger manifests itself especially in repetition. Someone who is seen punching another person in the face with the same motion over and over is in the grips of hot anger. Cold anger is controlled and focused. It enables us to function and act with awareness and decisiveness, without robbing us of rational thought. Obviously, if the goal is to defend oneself humanely, then cold anger rather than hot anger must be mastered.

One of the easiest techniques for mastering this potent force is to develop "the glare." The glare is a facial expression of focused ferocity. Practice by staring in the mirror. First, look relaxed and calm, then, as quickly as you can, switch to a fierce glare. Next, look timid and frightened, then switch to the glare. Practice this until you can feign any state of mind, then switch instantly to the glare. Notice that as you practice the glare, you will experience feelings of strength and intensity. This is the mind-body connection working for you. When you create the image of confident power with your face, your mind follows.

Author George Dillman exhibits "the glare" and "the shout" during training.

THE SHOUT

Nature has taught all creatures to use their voice as a deterrent against attack. That is why dogs growl, cats hiss, and badgers snarl. The voice is a powerful instrument of self-defense. For centuries, martial arts experts have cultivated the use of voice in the distinctive *kiai* (karate shout). This powerful shout helps the martial artist tap inner strength, while at the same time scaring and disorienting an opponent. As in the animal world, a strong *kiai* alone has caused many a would-be attacker to back down. However, people in general, and women in particular, find it very difficult to shout in this manner. The reason is social conditioning. The shout is innate, instinctive, but we have quieted nature with culture.

To reclaim this powerful natural weapon, begin by looking in a mirror glaring with ferocity. Take a deep breath, squeeze your buttocks muscles tightly, tighten your stomach, then drive a loud, guttural shout from your body using the muscles of your stomach and diaphragm. Specifically, we recommend that your shout come in the form of the word, "NO!" Be careful not to perform this more than a few times in any given practice session, as the shout can be stressful for the vocal cords.

After you have developed your shout, practice this drill with a partner. Stand with your back to a wall, and a bland expression on your face. Have a man walk towards you until it feels as if he has entered your personal space. Immediately bring your hands up in a non-confrontational manner, and say firmly, "Stop." Your partner is to stop for one or two seconds, then begin walking towards you again. Once he gets uncomfortably close, you are to bring the look of glare to your face and using your strongest shout, say, "NO!" This exercise will help you link the use of glare and shout to your feelings of threat and danger.

PARTNER PLAY

Partner play is a very important part of translating *Humane Pressure Point Self-Defense* skills from the book to the street. However, it is very clearly "play." Partner play should not feel competitive, but should be like a game. Once again, nature is the model. In the wild, all young animals play as a way of developing the survival and hunting skills they will need as adults. Similarly, human children play to learn and develop social skills. Partner play simply utilizes this natural learning methodology to ingrain self-defense skills.

Begin by playing the self-defense routines in this book. Have a partner simulate each attack, and you simulate each response. Make sure to play out the appropriate reactions to each move. So, if you simulate a strike to the Jaw Stun Point (S-5) your partner should stagger as if actually hit. For safety's sake, do not move too quickly, practicing at no more than 3/4-speed.

The next play drill is more difficult, but is an important step in the learning process. You begin by closing your eyes. While your eyes are shut, your partner will move in with a simulated attack. Once your partner is in "attack position," you open your eyes, and find some appropriate response. At first, your partner should move in slow motion, giving you time to solve the self-defense problem he is presenting. As you become better, you may pick up the rate of practice, but, again, never faster than 3/4-speed. Because you begin with your eyes shut, your brain is forced to quickly evaluate the situation and produce an appropriate response. This helps increase your reaction time in unpredictable situations.

TORSO DUMMY

One of the problems with partner play is that you cannot actually hit your partner, and this leaves out an important component of training. (A note here is in order: when studying under an instructor of Dillman Method *Humane Pressure Point Self-*

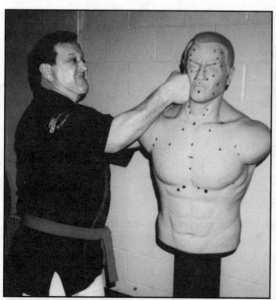 

The torso dummy is a valuable training tool. **B.O.B.**, from Century Martial Arts, is affectionately known as "George" because of its resemblance to author George Dillman. Similarly, the **Target Pro**, from ProLine, is known as "Virtual-Trav" because it resembles officer Travis Pobuda, who appears as an attacker in this book.

Defense, actually striking the pressure points in a controlled and supervised manner is part of the training method. However, as a matter of safety, we do not recommend that anyone practice this without proper instruction and supervision.) The torso dummy is a valuable tool which allows you to practice with actual contact. Unfortunately, torso dummies are somewhat expensive (ranging from about $150 up to $300). However, they are so helpful that professional pressure point experts routinely use them in practice and teaching. The two best torso dummies are the B.O.B. from Century Martial Arts (Midwest City, Oklahoma) and the Target-Pro from Pro-Line (Gatesville, TX).

The first thing to do with a torso dummy is exactly locate each of the vital targets and pressure points you know. It is very helpful to mark them with a pen, since this will help you to mentally fix their locations. Then, systematically practice striking each of the points and targets. Pay attention to the correct angle and method of attack. It is helpful to keep the torso dummy in a location you pass with frequency and to make a habit of attacking it whenever you go by. Another excellent way to practice is to have a partner call out points and vital targets for you to hit as quickly and accurately as you can. This is a powerful drill because it forces you to keep mentally aware and rationally in control while your are attacking pressure points.

The next drill can be very nerve-racking, and so it adds a realistic element of stress to your practice. In a darkened room (not pitch-black, simply dimly lit) stand with your eyes closed. Your partner positions the torso dummy nearby (the dummy can be removed from the base and held in the hands, or the whole thing can simply be moved around, as long as the base has not been weighted down). Then, standing behind the dummy, your partner is to shout. This is your cue to open your eyes and attack the dummy. Make sure to use glare, your shout, and multiple strikes to pressure points and vital targets.

This drill works for several reasons. For starters, a darkened room touches on our visceral fear of the dark, and fear is one of the over-riding experiences of self-defense. Second, your partner's shout both startles and tells you where to look for your attacker. This forces your brain to chose between the reflex to retreat from the frightening stimulus (the noise) and the need to move forward with your defense. Another aspect of this exercise is the darkness. In a darkened environment your eyes "see more slowly." This is literally true. In dim light it takes longer for the nerve impulses to travel from the eye to the brain. The rate of neural response is directly proportional to the intensity of the stimulus. Since dim light is not a strong stimulus, the optic nerve becomes sluggish in transmitting information. But, many self-defense situations develop in conditions of dim lighting, and this training method helps to prepare one for such encounters.

DESENSITIZATION

Confronting interpersonal violence is probably the most psychologically stressful experience the human organism can face (this is why the victims of interpersonal violence routinely suffer from some degree of post-traumatic stress disorder). Under the stress of a violent encounter, individuals will sometimes lose complete control: fully 1/4 will experience some form of bodily evacuation (urination, vomiting, defecation). Most will experience tunnel vision, auditory exclusion (a kind of selective hearing), and temporal distortion (time seems to slow down). The body can start to feel sluggish and uncooperative as adrenaline causes the extremities to shake uncontrollably. It is possible to lessen the degree of these responses by practicing desensitization exercises such as the one presented here. However, the following drill must be practiced with a trusted friend (do <u>not</u> do this with your spouse or loved-one).

Sit down with your training partner and have a nice conversation. At some point, your partner is to suddenly become irate, screaming obscenities at you, waving fists threateningly and so on. This must come without warning. As soon as this occurs, you are to adopt the fierce glare and shout, "Back off!" Or words to that effect. Your partner is to immediately comply, and then (<u>and this is critical</u>) should congratulate you on how you did, give you a "high-five" and generally praise your performance. This is classical psychological conditioning — stimulus-response-reward. It is designed to replace your present response to the threat of interpersonal violence (fear) with a new and desirable response (action, in this case the use of the glare and the shout).

During the course of an otherwise pleasant hour's conversation, you and your partner can alternate roles, each reacting to half a dozen or more tirades. At the end of the agreed upon time, spend a few minutes "debriefing" as you talk about your physical and emotional responses to the experience. If you find this exercise too stressful (it is far more difficult than reading about it would suggest) reduce the intensity by removing one of the elements. For example, you and your partner might limit the "assault" to verbal threats only, no physical actions. Or, you could use a kitchen timer as a signal for the "assault," in order to eliminate the element of surprise and give you a split-second of warning before your partner begins to act out the role. With time, however, the goal is to increase the level of stress in the drill so that you become <u>de</u>sensitized to threatening stimulus as a fear generator and <u>re</u>sensitized to threatening stimulus as an action initiator.

ABOVE: Kimberly Fritz (now, Kimberly Dillman) receiving the 1971 National Karate Champion trophy, presented by Robert Trias, Joe Lewis and Bill Wallace.

LEFT: Author George Dillman with his mother Betty.

Because of the changing face of modern combat, and the emerging role of the military in peace-keeping operations, this group of active duty U.S. Marines are training in Humane Pressure Point Self-Defense with Chris Thomas, Mickey Wittekiend, and Dusty Seale (back row).

Dusty Seale instructing marines in the method of striking down on the nose.

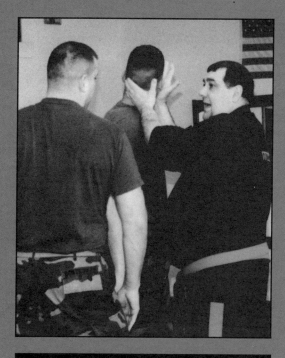

Mickey Wittekiend instructing marines in head-turning techniques.

BIBLIOGRAPHY & SOURCES

ACADEMY OF TRADITIONAL
CHINESE MEDICINE
AN OUTLINE OF CHINESE ACUPUNCTURE
Chan's Corporation, 1983

BEIJING COLLEGE OF TRADITIONAL
CHINESE MEDICINE, et. al
ESSENTIALS OF CHINESE ACUPUNCTURE
Pergamon Press, Ltd., 1981

DEADMAN, Peter, AL-KHAFAJI, Mazin,
BAKER, Kevin
A MANUAL OF ACUPUNCTURE
Journal of Chinese Medicine
Publications, 1998

De BECKER, Gavin
**THE GIFT OF FEAR: SURVIVAL SIGNALS
THAT PROTECT US FROM VIOLENCE**
Little, Brown and Co., 1997

DILLMAN, George A., THOMAS, Chris
**KYUSHO-JITSU: THE DILLMAN
METHOD OF PRESSURE POINT FIGHTING**
Dillman Karate International,
Publishers, 1992
**ADVANCED PRESSURE POINT FIGHTING OF
RYUKYU KEMPO**
Dillman Karate International,
Publishers, 1994
**ADVANCED PRESSURE POINT GRAPPLING
— TUITE´**
Dillman Karate International,
Publishers, 1995
LITTLE JAY LEARNS KARATE
Dillman Karate International,
Publishers, 1997
PRESSURE POINT KARATE MADE EASY
Dillman Karate International,
Publishers, 1999

GRANT, J. C. Boileau
GRANT'S ATLAS OF ANATOMY (6th ed.)
The Williams & Wilkins Co., 1972

GROSSMAN, Dave, Lt. Col. (Ret.)
**ON KILLING: THE PSYCHOLOGICAL COST
OF LEARNING TO KILL IN WAR &
SOCIETY**
Little, Brown and Co., 1996

GUYTON, Arthur C., M.D.
TEXTBOOK OF MEDICAL PHYSIOLOGY (7th ed.)
W.B. Saunders, Co, 1986

HOLLINSHEAD, W. Henry, Ph.D.
**ANATOMY FOR SURGEONS: VOLUME 1
THE HEAD AND THE NECK** (2nd ed.)
Harper & Row, Publishers, Inc., 1968

MILLER, Ronald D., M.D.
**ANESTHESIA: ATLAS OF REGIONAL
ANESTHESIA PROCEDURES** (5th ed.)
Churchill Livingstone, 2000

NETTER, Frank H., M.D.
ATLAS OF HUMAN ANATOMY
CIBA-GEIGY Ltd., 1989

QUINN, Peyton
**BOUNCER'S GUIDE TO BARROOM
BRAWLING**
Paladin Press, 1990

ROHEN, Johannes W., YOKOCHI, Chihiro,
LUTJEN-DRECOLL, Elke
COLOR ATLAS OF HUMAN ANATOMY (4th ed.)
Williams & Wilkins Co., 1998

SHANDONG MEDICAL COLLEGE &
SHANDONG COLLEGE OF TRADITIONAL
CHINESE MEDICINE
**ANATOMICAL ATLAS OF CHINESE
ACUPUNCTURE POINTS**
Pergamon Press, 1982

TAYLOR, Bob, WANNER, Randy
UNARMED AND FEARLESS (Video)
Tactical Response Solutions, 1994

SHANGHAI COLLEGE OF
TRADITIONAL MEDICINE
ACUPUNCTURE: A COMPREHENSIVE TEXT
Eastland Press, 1981

SMITHEE, Allen
ULTIMATE STREET BRAWLS (Video)
Reality Productions, Inc. 1997

WILSON-PAUWELS, AKESSON, STEWART
**CRANIAL NERVES: ANATOMY AND
CLINICAL COMMENTS**
B.C. Decker, Inc., 1988

ZARRILLI, Philip K.
**TO HEAL AND/OR TO HARM: THE VITAL
SPOTS IN TWO SOUTH INDIAN MARTIAL
TRADITIONS**
Journal of Asian Martial Arts,
Vol. 1, No. 1 & No. 2, 1992

KYUSHO-JITSU:
The Dillman Method of Pressure Point Fighting

by George A. Dillman
with Chris Thomas

272 pages, soft cover, $34.95
ISBN 0-9631996-1-7

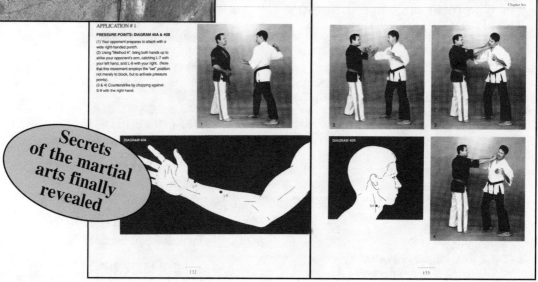

Secrets of the martial arts finally revealed

Kyusho-jitsu, or pressure point fighting, has long been a closely guarded secret of the martial arts. Taught to almost no one, the art was in danger of disappearing forever. In this revolutionary book, world famous karate instructor George A. Dillman with noted martial arts authority and writer Chris Thomas openly reveal the secrets of pressure point fighting to western martial artists of all styles. **KYUSHO-JITSU: The Dillman Method of Pressure Point Fighting** contains 272 pages of vital information, including the correct ways to apply common martial arts techniques that virtually every school teaches incorrectly, and methods of restoring energy to insure safe practice. Already considered a classic among martial arts books, it has forever changed the way traditional karate is understood.

"This kyusho-jitsu is a wonderful technique. I was also impressed by the unique methods of *kappo* (revival)."

Chosei Motobu, son of Choki Motobu and *soke* (inheritor) of Motobu-ryu karate-jitsu

Advanced Pressure Point Fighting of RYUKYU KEMPO

by George A. Dillman
with Chris Thomas

272 pages, soft cover, $34.95
ISBN 0-9631996-3-3

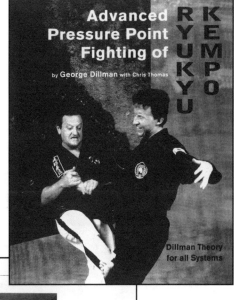

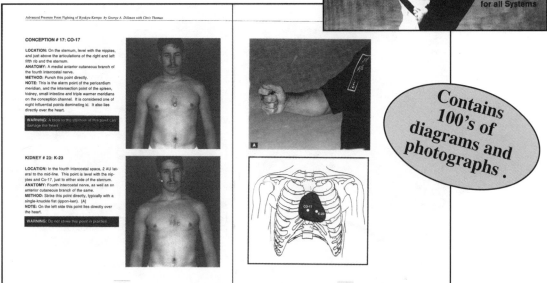

Contains 100's of diagrams and photographs.

The ancient secrets of the martial arts have been passed down through traditional routines called *kata* (forms). But, while the kata themselves have survived, the meaning of the movements is all but lost. In **Advanced Pressure Point Fighting of RYUKYU KEMPO**, world famous karate instructor George A. Dillman and noted martial arts authority and writer Chris Thomas unlock the secrets of these ancient methods. The book contains detailed information on the exact location and use of over 80 pressure points, a thorough explanation of pressure point theory, the complete pattern of the ancient kata Naihanchi, and a comprehensive analysis of its fighting secrets.

"Dillman's efforts have forced a generation of martial artists to reevaluate their understanding of kata."

Patrick McCarthy, karate historian and author of *BUBISHI: The Bible of Karate*

Advanced Pressure Point Grappling TUITE´

by George A. Dillman
with Chris Thomas

360 pages, soft cover, $39.95
ISBN 0-9631996-4-1

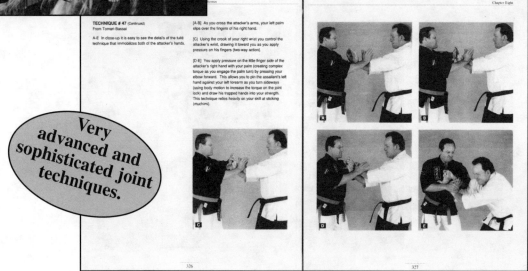

Very advanced and sophisticated joint techniques.

T uite´ is the art of devastating joint manipulation. These amazing methods allow a small person to easily control a much larger and stronger opponent. Tuite´ techniques use pressure points to weaken limbs and release joints. Combining tuite´ with pressure point strikes (kyusho-jitsu) creates a complete and comprehensive self-defense system that is adaptable to any circumstance. In **Advanced Pressure Point Grappling — TUITE´**, world famous karate instructor George A. Dillman and noted martial arts authority and writer Chris Thomas reveal the exact details of this amazing art. This profusely illustrated volume details the underlying principles of tuite´, the exact location and use of over 60 pressure points, and 50 clearly explained and easy to follow tuite´ techniques.

"Dillman is, without a doubt, a genius of the martial arts."
Richard Kim, Ph.D., karate master, historian and author of *The Weaponless Warriors*

Pressure Point Karate Made Easy

by George A. Dillman with Chris Thomas
144 pages, soft cover, $14.95
ISBN 1-889267-02-3

Originally written for young people as an introduction to authentic, old-style pressure point karate, **Pressure Point Karate Made Easy** has quickly become the preferred primer on the subject of kyusho-jitsu (pressure point fighting) for martial artists of all ages and skill levels. World famous karate instructor George A. Dillman and noted martial arts authority and writer Chris Thomas have crafted a book that clearly explains and illustrates the core principles of the original, but long-secret, methods of karate.

"Dillman's study and research of pressure point fighting have taken the martial arts to a higher level."

Leo Fong, kung fu master, author, action film producer, director and star.

Little Jay Learns Karate

Written by: Chris Thomas
Illustrated by: Dan Rosandich
Created by: George & Kimberly Dillman

48 pages, soft cover, $9.95
ISBN 1-889267-01-5

This delightful and thought-provoking story helps to introduce the ethical concepts which are a part of all traditional martial arts training. It provides the perfect entry for conversations between parents and children who are interested in studying karate. School teachers have found **Little Jay Learns Karate** to be especially useful for helping young students discover the joys of reading because the topic of karate draws their interest and wise story holds their attention.

"My nephew was thrilled with *Little Jay Learns Karate*. It's a fun book and a good introduction to the principles of the martial arts"

Michael Hauge, screenwriter, script consultant,
and author of *Writing Screenplays That Sell*.

Instructional Videos from
Dillman Karate International

Tape MS-1: The Science of Pressure Points
"Live" recording of the medical research done on pressure point techniques (discussed in Appendix One). You are there!

Tape H: Humane Pressure Point Self-Protection
George Dillman "Live," teaching a seminar to Chicago-area police officers and martial artists on Humane Pressure Point Tactics for Law Enforcement.

Tape FPO: For Police Only
In this tape, George Dillman and sergeant Bruce Fronk provide detailed instruction on the Humane Pressure Point Law Enforcement Techniques shown in chapter 5. The tape was produced in conjunction with this book

These three tapes are the video companions to the book
Humane Pressure Point Self-Defense
written by George Dillman with Chris Thomas.

Tape 19: Pure Knockouts
You will be amazed as George Dillman and his students demonstrate 75 effortless pressure point knockouts. This tape is for informational and entertainment purposes only!

For information and pricing for these and other videos and books, visit our website:

www.dillman.com
Over 45 Titles Available!